LINDA MACNEIL
Jewels of Glass

LINDA MACNEIL
Jewels of Glass

Davira S. Taragin
with
Ursula Ilse-Neuman

Museum of Glass, Tacoma, Washington
arnoldsche ART PUBLISHERS

Linda MacNeil: Jewels of Glass accompanies the exhibition of the same name organized by the Museum of Glass, Tacoma, Washington, on view from January 21 through October 1, 2017.

Museum of Glass
1801 Dock Street
Tacoma, Washington 98402
www.museumofglass.org

Arnoldsche Art Publishers
Olgastrasse 137
70180 Stuttgart, Germany
www.arnoldsche.com

Library of Congress Control Number:
2016028492

ISBN 978-3-89790-471-2

Printed in Germany

Publication coordinated and edited by
Terry Ann R. Neff
t.a. neff associates, inc.
Tucson, Arizona

TABLE OF CONTENTS

FOREWORD

Linda MacNeil and I first began a conversation about an exhibition in November 2013 at SOFA (Sculpture Objects Functional Art + Design), Chicago. We were attending a private party and had the great good fortune to sit together and, over the course of a marvelous dinner, plan the partnership that now culminates in *Linda MacNeil: Jewels of Glass*. For a number of years, I have been intrigued by MacNeil's sculptured compositions renowned for their exquisite craftsmanship and innovative use of materials and, of course, especially captivated by her inclusion of glass. Often described as miniature sculptures, MacNeil's work with its innovative incorporation of glass provides a groundbreaking opportunity for the Museum of Glass (MOG) to present its first exhibition of jewelry.

MacNeil's work has evolved over a career that now spans decades and reflects the influences and teachings of some of the most renowned jewelers and glass artists of the twentieth century. This includes the time spent under the tutelage of J. Fred Woell at the Haystack-Hinckley School of Crafts in Hinckley, Maine, and Dale Chihuly at the Rhode Island School of Design in Providence. Eschewing the social and political commentary commonplace in jewelry in the mid-century, MacNeil chose instead to find inspiration in the refined and enigmatic Art Deco period. She is especially inspired by the work of René Lalique, whose infinitely imaginative and naturally inspired works are an endless source of delight. It is indeed serendipitous that *Linda MacNeil: Jewels of Glass* is on view at the Museum of Glass at the same time as *Art Deco Glass from the David Huchthausen Collection*, which will provide a historical context in order to understand and appreciate this extraordinary creative style.

Linda MacNeil's place in the history of jewelry is elegantly explored in the essay by Ursula Ilse-Neuman, "Unmistakably MacNeil." Ilse-Neuman takes the reader through the evolution of jewelry in the twentieth century, from the Bauhaus movement to the importance of Alexander Calder, as well as the impact of the GI Bill and the role of prestigious schools such as the Rhode Island School of Design and the Rochester Institute of Technology, Rochester, New York, in fostering metalsmithing and jewelry along with other craft forms. Reaching all the way back to Ancient Egypt and then to Venice, Ilse-Neuman traces the use of glass as a material worthy of figuring in personal adornment. Her essay serves as a contextual and historical backdrop to MOG guest curator Davira S. Taragin's essay, "Linda MacNeil: Defying Categorization."

Taragin provides a thorough and deep analysis of MacNeil's career, influences, and techniques. She reveals the impact of such seminal figures as John ("Jack") Prip, whose Danish stylistic immersion resonated with MacNeil, as did the knowledge she gained from her frequent trips to Cristallerie Daum in France early in her career. Against the backdrop of the Studio Glass movement, Taragin skillfully weaves an interconnection between the Studio Glass world and the evolution of MacNeil's series, which were, and are, profiled in major exhibitions around the country. Taragin pays attention to the impact of Art Deco on MacNeil's aesthetic and also includes reference to the inspiration of Ancient Egyptian and Celtic art forms in her work.

The Museum of Glass is deeply honored to present *Linda MacNeil: Jewels of Glass* and the new scholarship so eloquently expressed in this book by Taragin and Ilse-Neuman. We are confident that the exhibition and this accompanying publication will provide enjoyment and a new understanding of the Studio practitioner of jewelry in the twentieth and twenty-first centuries, as well as MacNeil's central role in this narrative. In particular, the Museum of Glass would like to thank Linda MacNeil for her graciousness, generosity, and humor throughout this process. She is a fine artist and consummate craftswoman. MacNeil's concern for those who wear her art is reflected in the care she takes in creating unique pieces that complement each patron's personality and physical presence and, in turn, mirror her own positive and warm outlook on life.

It is with gratitude that I acknowledge the museum's trustees and its executive director, Deborah Lenk, for their support and encouragement of the presentation of this unusual exhibition to our public. Special thanks go to Davira S. Taragin, who not only contributed an essay reflecting exacting research, attention to detail, and extensive original documentation of Linda MacNeil's career but was responsible for organizing the exhibition for MOG. As guest curator, she has been involved in every aspect of the project, from finalizing the checklist, writing the labels, and installing the works to advising on publishing options and photography. We also thank editor and publication coordinator Terry Ann R. Neff of t.a. neff associates, Tucson, Arizona, for her tireless oversight of all stages of this publication, and Dirk Allgaier, managing director of Arnoldsche Art Publishers, Stuttgart, our copublishers. MOG's skilled and passionate curatorial and education departments also deserve acknowledgment: Rebecca Engelhardt, collections and exhibitions manager; Katie Buckingham, assistant curator; Lynette Martin, exhibition designer; Amanda Brebner, rights and reproductions specialist; Bonnie Wright, curator of education and community engagement; and Elisabeth Emerson, education coordinator. Special recognition is also extended to the numerous collectors who loaned to this exhibition and who have invested in Linda MacNeil's career and accomplishments. We deeply appreciate their willingness to forgo wearing their jewelry for an extended period to showcase MacNeil's extraordinary career. And we are tremendously grateful for the generous support of Marian and Russell Burke, Larry and Klara Silverstein and the Silverstein Family Trust, Guendolen Carkeek Plestcheef Fund for the Decorative and Design Arts, Diane and Jerome Phillips, Art Alliance for Contemporary Glass, Farah and John Palmer, and Sharon Karmazin.

Susan Warner
Artistic Director
Museum of Glass

SPONSORS

Marian and Russell Burke

Larry and Klara Silverstein and the Silverstein Family Trust

Guendolen Carkeek Plestcheef Fund for the Decorative and Design Arts

ARTSFUND

Diane and Jerome Phillips

Art Alliance for Contemporary Glass

A A C G

Farah and John Palmer

Sharon Karmazin

ACKNOWLEDGMENTS

When Linda MacNeil approached me in 2014 to organize her first scholarly exhibition and monograph for the Museum of Glass, I agreed enthusiastically to do it because she is one of a number of important Studio artists who have not been the subject of in-depth examination. I was delighted that the Museum of Glass has chosen, as part of its mission, to provide a venue for the documentation of the careers of such American artists whose contributions to contemporary glass have not gotten the attention they deserve. While I had long been aware of MacNeil's role in late twentieth and early twenty-first-century decorative arts, I hoped that my study of her career would provide further insight into the blurring of the boundaries of art, craft, and design that has marked this exciting period—a subject that has interested me throughout my career. MacNeil's position is particularly distinctive as she has always been identified with two worlds—glass and jewelry—unlike most Studio Craft artists, such as ceramicists Peter Voulkos and Betty Woodman or furniture-maker Wendell Castle, who are immediately classified as leaders in their respective fields.

I would never have been able to accomplish this research without the warm, dedicated assistance, cooperation, and friendship of Mary Beth Kreiner, librarian, from the Cranbrook Academy of Art Library in Bloomfield Hills, Michigan. Along with her colleagues Judy Dyki, library director, and Elizabeth Dizik, library assistant, Kreiner continually over the past months went to sources all around the country to obtain often obscure references and announcements that were critical to construct MacNeil's career and evolution. Early on, Jessica Shaykett, librarian, and Dulcey Heller, library assistant, of the American Craft Council Library in Minneapolis, similarly provided invaluable assistance in making available much of the essential information that served as the basis of this study. Alison Huftalen, head librarian, Toledo Museum of Art, Toledo, Ohio; Elizabeth Hylen, reference and education librarian, Rakow Research Library, Corning Museum of Glass, Corning, New York; and Karen L. Morgan, librarian emerita, Mardigian Library, University of Michigan – Dearborn also deserve thanks for their contributions.

Extensive museum archives were made available by Nicholas Bell, formerly at the Renwick Gallery of the Smithsonian American Art Museum, Washington, DC, and Marguerite Hergesheimer of that same institution; Laura Cotton and Timothy A. Ammons, Alfred Berkowitz Gallery, Mardigian Library, University of Michigan – Dearborn; Samantha DeTillio and Barbara Gifford, Museum of Arts and Design, New York; Bruce Pepich and Laura Grayson, Racine Art Museum, Racine, Wisconsin; Emily Zilber and summer intern Christina Warzecha, Museum of Fine Arts, Boston; and Cindi Strauss, The Museum of Fine Arts, Houston.

I also wish to express gratitude to the following individuals and institutions for their invaluable assistance: Ronald Abramson, Jane Adlin, Howard Ben Tré, Jamie Bennett, David Bernstein, Susan Cummins, Mark Del Vecchio, Joan Einbender and Joe Scicluna, Helen W. Drutt English, Arline Fisch, Barbara Heinrich, Erling Heistad, Giselle Huberman, Colleen and John Kotelly, Beverly Kostrinsky, Ellie Lainer, Nanette L. Laitman and Patti M. Richards, Lynn Leff, Andrew M. Lewis, Alex Mayer, Anna and Joe Mendel, Bella Neyman, Joan Ochroch, Diane and Jerome Phillips, Donna Schneier, Klara Silverstein, Paul J. Smith, Ruth Summers, Gustavo Tirado, and William Warmus. My institutional colleagues include Emily Acker, Fine Arts Museums of San Francisco; Elisabeth Agro, Philadelphia Museum of Art; Dan Blask, Massachusetts Cultural Council; Abbey Chamberlain Brach, Los Angeles County Museum of Art; Josephine Burri, The University of the Arts; Bruce Chao, Rhode Island School of Design; Diane Charbonneau, The Montreal Museum of Fine Arts; Sharon Church, The University of the Arts; Ken Clark, Chihuly Studio; Debbie Clason, Habatat Galleries; Katie Clausen, Carnegie Museum of Art; JoAnne and Libby Cooper, Mobilia Gallery; Lori Dempsey, Smithsonian Institution Traveling Exhibition Service; Iris Eichenberg, Cranbrook Academy of Art; Rebecca Elliot, The Mint Museum; Scott Erbes, Speed Museum; Maxine Frankel, Maxine and Stuart Frankel Foundation for Art; Gail Garee, Hawk Galleries; Susan Gogan, Wheaton Arts and Cultural Center; Nancy Grinnell, formerly at the Newport Art Museum; Corey Hampson, Habatat Galleries; Sherry Hawk, National Liberty Museum; Douglas Heller, Heller Gallery; Honee A. Hess, Worcester Center for Crafts; Scott Jacobson, Scott Jacobson Gallery; Kate Jordan, Urban Expositions; Pamela Figenshow Koss, Glass Art Society; Elizabeth Le, Hunter Museum of American Art; Emily Leischner, Philadelphia Museum of Art; Karen Lorene, Facèré Jewelry Art Gallery; Rod McCormick, The University of the Arts; Molly McIntosh, Imago Galleries; Rosie Mills, Los Angeles County Museum of Art; Nancy O'Meara, Philadelphia Museum of Art; Tina Oldknow, formerly at the Corning Museum of Glass; Robin Quigley, Rhode Island School of Design; Suzanne Ramljak, *Metalsmith* magazine; Tom Riley, formerly of Thomas R. Riley Galleries; Kim Saul and Jim Schantz, Schantz Galleries; Lindsey Scott, Habatat Galleries; Barry Shifman, Virginia Museum of Fine Arts; Emily E. Smith, Corning Museum of Glass; Benjamin Teague, Maxine and Stuart Frankel Foundation for Art; Bobbye Tigerman, Los Angeles County Museum of Art; Rebecca Tilghman, The Metropolitan Museum of Art; Jane Weinke, Leigh Yawkey Woodson Art Museum; Pamela Annarilli Weichmann, Wheaton Arts and Cultural Center; Diane C. Wright, Chrysler Museum of Art; Joey Yates, Kentucky Museum of Art and Craft; and Sherry Zambrano, Bass Museum of Art.

Over my career, I have witnessed the work of several professionals whom I have held in the highest esteem. I was particularly thrilled to have been able to assemble them as the project team for this show. Terry Ann R. Neff of t.a. neff associates, inc. has performed at her customary exceptional level in the editing and coordination of the publication, providing both invaluable friendship and the highest level of expertise as the team maneuvered through the myriad of queries that accompanies such an endeavor. Bill Truslow (www.truslowphoto.com) has over the years regularly been called upon by Linda MacNeil to document her oeuvre; I wish to thank him for making so many of his images available for use.

Since I have previously worked with Michael Tropea, I invited him to join the team; he provided outstanding photography and much-appreciated advice. The images of these two photographers are augmented with those by John Carlano, Susie Cushner, Christian Lunardi of Lunardi Photography, Charles Mayer, and PD Rearick. I am most grateful to each of them for their sensitive contributions to this monograph. Ursula Ilse-Neuman and I have known each other for many years, but this project offered us a first opportunity to work together. I come away from it having discovered an exceptional scholar and kindred spirit with whom I hope to share ideas for years to come. Finally, I want to thank Dirk Allgaier, Marion Boschka, and the team at Arnoldsche Art Publishers for their interest and support of this project. It has been an enormous pleasure to work with them; it is particularly meaningful that this publication has been chosen as part of Arnoldsche's highly esteemed series on contemporary jewelers.

Above all, I wish to thank Dan Dailey, who regularly provided personal and professional perspectives that led me to investigate new directions; Ken Gray of Dailey/MacNeil Studios, who assisted in many aspects of the preparation of this exhibition; and Susan Warner, artistic director of the Museum of Glass, who, through this exhibition, gave me an opportunity to continue my longtime research into contemporary crafts; I greatly appreciate her support. I would also like to extend my warmest appreciation to Rebecca Engelhardt, collections and exhibition manager at the Museum of Glass, who diligently worked on the execution of the various responsibilities inherent to exhibition organization, which here included overseeing with the artist the publication's photography. Finally, I wish to thank Linda MacNeil, who worked tirelessly alongside me throughout this entire project. I sincerely hope that our efforts in this exhibition and monograph will help guarantee her place within the pantheon of innovative American jewelers of the twentieth and early twenty-first centuries.

Davira S. Taragin
Guest Curator

LINDA MACNEIL: DEFYING CATEGORIZATION

Davira S. Taragin

Linda MacNeil is not the typical jeweler. MacNeil, who works without maintaining academic affiliations, has inserted her own voice into contemporary American jewelry as an innovator transforming glass into proxies for precious gemstones. A pioneer over her forty-and-counting-year career, this New England native has selected the necklace as her primary form. Uniting glass—hot-worked, industrially fabricated, cast, or slumped—which is then polished and/or acid-polished, with hand-manipulated metal stock and, more recently, with precious gems, she explores materiality and methodology. She uses historical precedent as a jumping off point to make wearable statements that unite a powerful palette with softened geometric and organic form.

MacNeil's visually exquisite and technically sophisticated work straddles two worlds—Studio Glass and Studio Jewelry. It is about adornment rather than narrative, one of the most frequently identified themes in America's art jewelry today. In fact, MacNeil is not definitively identified with art jewelry because she emphasizes craftsmanship rather than content.[1] Similarly, her work does not fit well contextually alongside nonfunctional glass sculpture. Nonetheless, MacNeil has overcome these obstacles of categorization to find her place as a significant contributor to decorative arts and crafts in the late twentieth and twenty-first centuries.

One factor that influences analyses of MacNeil and her career is that her husband is Dan Dailey (United States, born 1947), one of today's leading glass sculptors. On the one hand, MacNeil and Dailey each have their own distinctive aesthetic. Unlike MacNeil, Dailey focuses on the narrative, incorporating recognizable imagery into statements ranging from nonfunctional sculptures (see Ilse-Neuman, Figure 3) to monumental functional forms, such as chandeliers and wall sconces. Yet, MacNeil has acknowledged the significance of the relationship, stating, "Dan's presence in my life is very important .... I feel very lucky because I know that I would not be as good an artist without the constant exchange with him."

Dailey's involvement in MacNeil's career was more pronounced at the beginning of their relationship. The two met in 1974 when she was his student in a ceramics elective at Boston's Massachusetts College of Art. Aware of her strong interest in metalwork and her keen desire to succeed as an artist, Dailey took special interest in his young protégée. He introduced her to the potential of glass, the importance of drawing as part of the creative process, and the role of series in developing ideas. A graduate of the Rhode Island School of Design (RISD) in Providence, Dailey brought MacNeil's work to the attention of John ("Jack") Prip

(United States, 1922–2009), who founded RISD's BFA and MFA programs in jewelry and metalsmithing, which led to her acceptance into its undergraduate program. The two years MacNeil spent at RISD proved more formative than her previous studies at Philadelphia College of Art (PCA) (September 1972–May 1973) and Massachusetts College of Art (MassArt) (September 1973–May 1974), even though master metalsmith Olaf Skoogfors (United States, born Sweden, 1930–1975) was still a presence at PCA. MacNeil received her BFA from RISD in 1976.

Today, MacNeil and Dailey share a commonality of working in both glass and metal, a love of certain artistic periods including Art Deco, and a fascination with technical execution. Because of their respective expertise in metal and glass, much has been written about their fabricating parts for each other's artwork. However, their relationship is much more about being "soulmates,"[2] sharing information, and offering each other helpful critiques. His acquaintances in the glass world have become hers, so they often have the same patrons and galleries; they have frequently exhibited and lectured together. Similarly, since MacNeil has never been interested in blowing glass herself but prefers the cold-working processes, such as cutting, shaping, and polishing, Dailey and those artists who sometimes blow components for his compositions have at times fabricated hot-worked elements for MacNeil.[3] Perhaps because of these associations, MacNeil has been positioned more in the contemporary glass world than in contemporary jewelry.

BEGINNINGS (1970S THROUGH 1985): TOWARD INTERNATIONAL RECOGNITION

In addition to Dailey, MacNeil often cites the strong influence that other members of her immediate family, including her grandparents, have exerted on the development of her career. Also, makers whom she met during her formative years played significant roles in defining MacNeil's direction. By age twelve, MacNeil regularly frequented the jewelry studio of Dartmouth College's Hopkins Center in Hanover, New Hampshire, headed by Cranbrook Academy of Art alumnus Erling Heistad (United States, born 1939). Heistad mentored her, advancing her jewelry skills. As a result, by the time MacNeil was a teenager, she was fabricating jewelry and selling it on the streets of Hanover.

Heistad also was responsible for MacNeil's long-standing friendship with the highly respected jeweler J. Fred Woell (United States, 1934–2015) (see Ilse-Neuman, Figure 2). With the help of Frances Merritt (United States, 1914–2001), then director of the renowned Haystack Mountain School of Crafts in Deer Isle, Maine, Heistad founded in 1969 the short-lived Haystack-Hinckley School of Crafts in Hinckley, Maine, for teenagers intent upon careers in the crafts. MacNeil was accepted into the program's 1971 summer session, where she registered for a jewelry course taught by Woell.[4] Today, MacNeil recalls that even though she had not then heard of Woell, the class proved "a great boost for me because he [Woell] was a friendly man, well-known for his art jewelry."[5] While Woell's aesthetic had little immediate impact on her, MacNeil came away from that experience with three career-defining revelations: reaffirmation of the importance of good craftsmanship, a focus on one-of-a-kind jewelry over production, and a new mentor. Woell continued to monitor MacNeil's career. He invited her to Boston University's School of Artisanry in 1981 to be a visiting artist. He also wrote a glowing review of one of her first solo gallery exhibitions for *Metalsmith* magazine.[6]

At PCA and MassArt, MacNeil came into peripheral contact with such teaching greats as Skoogfors and furniture-maker Dan Jackson (United States, 1938–1995), both of whom she wished to emulate. At RISD, however, her contact with its renowned teaching staff was considerably more direct. For example, through an independent study project that she proposed, she became well acquainted with Dale Chihuly (United States, born 1941), Dailey's former graduate professor, who gave her a new perspective on professionalism. John Prip, however, had the greatest influence on MacNeil. She found his Danish background "exotic" and recalls that he went through the studios after hours rearranging her work as well as that of the others. He talked more than demonstrated, preferring discussions about aesthetics over process. His functional, modernist forms, executed largely in pewter, with clean, simplified geometries whose roots lay in the podlike forms of nature, strongly appealed to the young MacNeil; today, she feels that her mature aesthetic of softened geometric forms reflects Prip's influence. In fact, the essentials of MacNeil's mature aesthetic—her interest in functionalism, mechanisms, symmetry, and even color—were in place by the time that she had graduated from RISD.

The years immediately after graduation were critical for MacNeil. She moved in with Dailey. Initially, they lived in Roslindale, Massachusetts, where a small bedroom of their apartment served as MacNeil's metalworking studio. In 1977, they moved to a house in Amesbury, Massachusetts, where there was room for her to do metalworking, but she had to use the facilities at Massachusetts College of Art for glass fabrication until cold-working equipment and kilns could be installed in the basement of their home. MacNeil and Dailey were married in 1978. Brief employment at Old Newbury Crafters in Amesbury, Massachusetts that same year made MacNeil realize that she did not enjoy working for others. A year earlier, she had accompanied Dailey on the first, for her, of four trips over much of the next decade to Cristallerie Daum in France, a glasshouse known for its pâte de verre. MacNeil never had a formal relationship with Daum; however, there she received in-depth knowledge about the material, its fabrication techniques, and its coloristic potential. She also took advantage of the facilities and the assistance of Daum's employees to have elements cast for a series of sculptural vases she completed in the early 1980s. Most significantly, she was given scrap Daum glass that she incorporated into her jewelry well into the next century.

MacNeil has always enjoyed mixing metal with other materials. She began experimenting with acrylics and then ebony and ivory, but by 1978, following Dailey's lead, she became intrigued with Vitrolite, an architectural glass popular in the United States from the 1930s through the early 1950s. Vitrolite figures prominently in MacNeil's first two major series, the "Elements" jewelry and the hand mirrors, both of which confirmed that she had found her own voice.[7]

"Elements" essentially presents a funky, almost Pop[8] approach to the traditional, symmetrically balanced, beaded necklace. According to MacNeil, who

1 Linda MacNeil. *Necklace No. 6* from the "Elements" series, 1979. Plate glass, Vitrolite glass, and 14k yellow gold. 6 11/16 x 5 1/2 x 7/8 inches (17 x 14 x 2.3 cm) (closed). Collection of the Victoria and Albert Museum, London, gift of the artist. Photo © Victoria and Albert Museum

considers the term "bead" pejorative, "the series … [is] based on classic arrangements of components that hang connected around the neck."[9] The cut and polished Vitrolite (see Plate 5), plate or hot-worked glass—and cast glass in the early 1980s—are frequently arranged in repeat patterns and connected, in some manner, by gold tubing, rods, wire, and sheet stock that MacNeil hand-manipulated (see Plate 6). Silver figures rarely in MacNeil's mature compositions because it was difficult to clean when juxtaposed with the glass. MacNeil's goal here was not to explore properties of glass but simply to create playful, wearable compositions. Even at this early stage, her knowledge of Art Deco is evident. For example, her study of the oeuvre of the Deco master René Lalique (France, 1860–1945) taught her that acid-polishing the glass (dipping it in hydrofluoric acid) produced a satiny finish; this technique became an essential part of her practice.[10]

Necklace and Bracelet (Plate 1 A–B)—one of her few such sets—demonstrates that the formula for the "Elements" series was in place early on. Here, the large, polished glass beads are essentially softly rounded cylinders formed by drilling sheets of clear plate glass and then drilling them a second time so that a hand-woven sterling silver chain can be threaded through. Decorative rivets keep the glass from moving, guaranteeing comfort and wearability. The chain testifies to the artist's thorough grounding in metalwork: woven wire techniques were popular at the time because of the creative output and writings of the metalsmith Arline Fisch (United States, born 1931).[11]

As the 1980s progressed, MacNeil's "Elements" necklaces, which resemble "pieces of candy"[12] (see Plate 9), became increasingly dense with greater color contrasts. As the glass components became more prominent, the metalwork was

2 Linda MacNeil. *Hand Mirror No. 7*, 1980. Hot-worked glass, Vitrolite glass, and pewter. 12 x 6 x 2 inches (30.5 x 15.2 x 5.1 cm). Collection of Anne and Ronald Abramson. Photo by Susie Cushner.

3 Linda MacNeil. *Plate Glass Vase No. 2*, 1982. Vitrolite glass, plate glass, and 24k gold–plated brass. 15 x 6 x 6 inches (38.1 x 15.2 x 15.2 cm). Courtesy of the artist. Photo by Susie Cushner.

less visible. In 1985, the introduction of geometrically shaped granite components (see Plate 11) injected a color restraint that would continue into the early 1990s. One "Elements" necklace was included in the critical 1981 exhibition *Good as Gold: Alternative Materials in American Jewelry*, organized by the Smithsonian Institution Traveling Exhibition Service. The exhibition documented, for the first time, American jewelers who echoed their European counterparts and worked with nontraditional materials. Another necklace was accessioned by London's Victoria and Albert Museum in 1988 (Figure 1). However, MacNeil's hand mirrors, an outgrowth of her studies at RISD, brought more immediate recognition, primarily from the glass world. Created largely between 1978 and 1981, some parts were actually fabricated in the North Carolina studio of pioneering glassmaker Harvey Littleton (United States, 1922–2013), where MacNeil briefly worked. The series evolved from more traditional formats, some of which were intended to be wall-hung (see Figure 2),[13] into whimsical objects for the tabletop that are more mechanical space-age sculpture—reflecting popular culture at the time—than functional. *Hand Mirror No. 15* (Plate 3) is an assemblage of interconnected, geometric volumes set at angles to one another and topped with two propellerlike Vitrolite bars. The mirror, while reflective, provides only limited visibility. Its handle, which is not readily identifiable, consists of commercial glass tubing into which small plate-glass cylinders have been stacked to create an Art Deco–inspired linear motif that appears frequently in MacNeil's work.

The hand mirrors were the subject of MacNeil's first solo show in a New York gallery in 1980.[14] One was chosen for inclusion in The Corning Museum of Glass's

New Glass Review, the highly respected annual publication that assessed developments in contemporary glass. A second, which featured a hot-worked glass handle fabricated by Dailey (Plate 4), was purchased that year by the Corning Museum for its permanent collection—a major triumph for the emerging artist.[15] This success was augmented when MacNeil's work was featured in *American Craft* magazine's February–March 1980 "Portfolio" section profiling up-and-coming talent.[16]

As MacNeil became more confident about working with glass and started to develop a context for the works that she was seeing by such talented figures as Howard Ben Tré (United States, born 1949), Stanislav Libenský (Czechoslovakia, 1921–2002) and Jaroslava Brychtová (Czechoslovakia, born 1924), Klaus Moje (Germany, 1936–2016), and František Vízner (Czechoslovakia, 1936–2011),[17] she began to explore in jewelry as well as nonfunctional sculptural forms the inherent nature of the material: its transparency, translucency, opacity, and reflective and refractive qualities. Polishing the glass to a high gloss joined acid-polishing as a necessary step of her fabrication process.

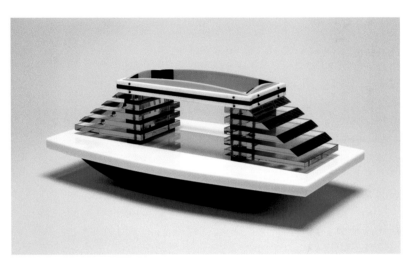

4   Linda MacNeil. *Abstract Vessel No. 1*, 1984. Vitrolite glass, plate glass, and brass. 7 3/16 x 17 3/4 x 9 15/16 inches (18.3 x 45.1 x 25.2 cm).
Collection of Maxine and Stuart Frankel, private collection.
Photo by PD Rearick.

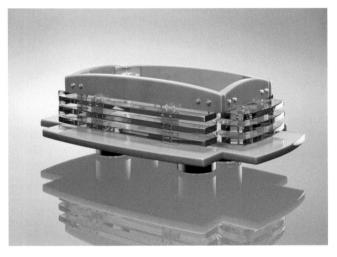

5   Linda MacNeil. *Plate Glass Vessel No. 5*, 1983. Vitrolite glass, plate glass, and 24k gold–plated brass. 4 1/4 x 11 1/2 x 8 inches (10.8 x 29.2 x 20.3 cm).
Collection of Beverly and Samuel Kostrinsky.
Photo by Susie Cushner.

Between 1981 and 1986, using as a point of departure the metal vessels of her RISD days, MacNeil executed several series of tabletop sculptures consisting of sections of Vitrolite, plate glass, or pâte de verre, and, later, granite, joined with screws and metal rivets—evidence of her interest in mechanisms—rather than the adhesives popular among glass sculptors at the time. This body of work started as vases (see Figure 3) that critics said resembled a "take-out box"[18] and evolved within a short time into other formats, such as miniature architectural statements (see Figure 4) and horizontally elongated architectonic vessels (see Plate 10).

One vessel (Figure 5) was featured in *The International Design Yearbook 1985/86*, edited by the renowned postmodernist architect Robert A. M. Stern (United States, born 1939).[19] When exhibited at such prestigious venues as New York's Heller Gallery and Habatat Galleries of Lathrup Village, Michigan, or at the *Sculptural Glass* exhibition organized in conjunction with the 1983 Glass Art Society conference in Tucson, Arizona, these sculptures were well received by dealers, critics, and glass collectors alike.[20] They continue to draw praise today.[21]

"Lucent Lines" is the series that brought MacNeil the ultimate in critical international acclaim: an article and cover image in the highly respected German magazine *Neues Glas*.[22] The "Lucent Lines" necklaces continued the concept of the "Elements" series in that both are based upon the symmetrically balanced, beaded necklace. In both series, each glass or metal part fills both a structural and an aesthetic need and demonstrates MacNeil's rationalist approach to design—a legacy, perhaps, of her grandfather, who was a well-respected architect. However, the "Lucent Lines" necklaces are more formal and deal entirely with issues of transparency. They exhibit MacNeil's penchant for the geometric, highly architectonic vocabulary that she learned from studying the French Art Deco designs of the House of Mauboussin and designer Jean Fouquet (France, 1899–1994) (see Ilse-Neuman, Figures 6 and 8).

The series' basic motif is three holes drilled into the glass; 14k yellow gold tubing is used to form the chain and the linkages between the glass components and the chain. The complexity demonstrates MacNeil's superior craftsmanship and fastidious attention to detail. For example, in the masterpiece of the series of thirty-four necklaces, *Necklace No. 4* (Plate 8), three small pieces of tubing that create linear patterns are inserted into the clear glass cylinders and rectangular shapes of drilled plate glass, subdividing them into four vertical sections that provide a counterpoint to the horizontality of the larger glass components.

Necklace No. 4, which was the cover image for a 1985 *Neues Glas* issue, was completed two years after she began working on the series. Since MacNeil's series do not progress chronologically and she might spend years working on a design, she is often able to create a tour de force early in a body of work. She continued the "Lucent Lines" series until 2008, subconsciously vacillating between an emphasis on metalwork and glass, as she has done throughout her career. In *Necklace Number 14* (Plate 22), for example, lengths of hand-manipulated linear gold tubing joined by small circular jump rings dominate the composition, framing the small, faceted glass forms and enhancing their resemblance to gemstones.

TRANSITIONING INTO MATURITY
(1985–2000)

The second half of the 1980s and the first years of the 1990s proved a transitional period for MacNeil. Health issues prevented her from fabricating heavy, nonfunctional sculptures; jewelry became the most viable alternative. Then, in 1988, MacNeil and Dailey purchased a large, early nineteenth-century farm in rural New Hampshire, which they converted into a living and studio space. They completed most of the studio area in two years, then turned to the living quarters; in 1992, they moved in. Even though a visit in 1987 from the British master Diana Hobson,[23] who is credited with the revival of pâte de verre among Studio Glass artists, had convinced MacNeil to continue her own efforts, the area for its fabrication was not finished until 1995. At the same time, MacNeil and Dailey's children, Allison and Owen, were still very young. Between construction and parenting, MacNeil's creative time was limited.

During these years, MacNeil was included in two highly prestigious jewelry exhibitions organized by the American Craft Museum (now New York's Museum of Arts and Design), *Jewelry USA* (1984–86) and *American Jewelry Now* (1985–87), and in surveys of contemporary craft, such as the American Craft Museum's *Poetry of the Physical* (1986–88) and *Contemporary Craft and the Saxe Collection* (1993–95), organized by the Toledo Museum of Art in Toledo, Ohio. In general, however, her aggressive pursuit of shows during the late 1980s and early 1990s declined. Also, MacNeil stopped attending the conferences organized by the Society of North American Goldsmiths and Glass Art Society because she did not see their professional relevance. Nonetheless, she remained prolific and produced such iconic series as the "Neck Collars."

The highly sculptural "Neck Collars" were her immediate response to her inability physically to make nonfunctional sculptures. Begun around 1986, they are quintessential investigations of geometric form, balanced "with some organic softness."[24] Best known are the round versions (see Plate 13), in which two symmetrically shaped pieces of textured glass are screwed on top of similarly shaped, slightly larger disks of 24k gold–plated brass and then hinged at the bottom. Earlier in her career, MacNeil had found that plating brass with 24k gold enabled her to achieve a satiny finish that complemented the acid-polishing. Adopting the technique in many of her sculptures, she also found it helped her achieve a coloristic "balance"[25] between the metal and the glass in some of her jewelry.

Triangular[26] and rectangular torques followed, with the glass pendant centrally situated within the metal framework. In subsequent years, she returned to the circular format, either screwing the glass element into the metal of the collar (see Plate 15) or embedding it with an adhesive within a bezellike form within the metalwork (Plate 16). Since wearability is one of MacNeil's primary concerns, she always wears her jewelry herself in the studio before offering it for sale. She observed, "The flat, circular disk-shaped 'Neck Collars' do not … conform around the shoulders and neck; therefore, they are more versatile to different body shapes." However, she found over the years that only some women could wear them comfortably.

Inspired by ancient Celtic torques, the "Neck Collars" symbolize a major evolution in MacNeil's work. For instance, the glass of *Neck Collar Ensemble No. 1* (Plate 12 A–C) is no longer strung as beads but is instead cut into geometric forms resembling gemstones—reminiscent of Art Deco master Fouquet's designs. This change in approach, reiterated in such other works as *Collar No. 10* (Plate 16), was noticed immediately by critics[27] and may have led then contemporary glass curator Susanne K. Frantz at The Corning Museum of Glass in Corning, New York, to recommend *Neck Collar Ensemble No. 1* for acquisition after seeing it in several gallery exhibitions, including one at the Helen Drutt Gallery in Philadelphia.

It also may have been what led Helen W. Drutt English to regularly exhibit MacNeil's work in her gallery in the late 1980s. Considered the "dean of the jewelry field,"[28] Drutt English showed avant-garde American and European jewelry as well as works in other craft media in her Philadelphia gallery beginning in 1973 and later in New York. Drutt English first exhibited MacNeil's work in 1979; her solo show of 1988, which highlighted this new work, represents just one of the many instances over the years where the respected gallerist, curator, and crafts scholar has championed MacNeil's art.[29] In fact, as recently as 2006, Drutt English asked MacNeil to participate in her innovative traveling exhibition *Challenging the Chatelaine!*, co-organized with Helsinki's Designmuseo.

Even though in MacNeil's next major series, the "Mirrored Glass" necklaces, she returned to the beaded necklace format of the "Elements" and "Lucent Lines" series, it represents the next logical progression in having glass substituted for gemstones. For example, the repetitive, faceted glass pyramids of *Necklace No. 1* (Plate 18), which alternate with commercially produced 14k yellow gold balls, resemble very large, dazzling diamonds. Here, using a technique first explored in *Collar No. 12* (Plate 17), MacNeil substituted plate-glass mirror for plate glass—to bring out "the most brilliant light reflections and refractions."

Stylistically, *Necklace No. 1* is a tour de force. At first glance, it recalls the fine jewelry of Harry Winston (United States, 1896–1978),[30] which MacNeil cited as a source of inspiration at that time. Studio Glass collector Anna Mendel, the owner of this necklace, observed that whenever she wears it, complete strangers come over to talk. Although they never ask her about it, they never take their eyes from it.[31] MacNeil herself was so delighted with the outcome of this technique that a variation on the process became her modus operandi. From 2001 onward, she laminated clear plate glass to thin sheets of colored glass and then to mirror, increasing the luminosity of the glass and, more importantly, obliterating the presence of the wearer's body through the glass.

Even with the introduction of these two new series, MacNeil was concerned about sales, which she began to equate with success. After exhibiting with the Helen Drutt Gallery in Philadelphia and New York in the late 1980s, in the early 1990s she joined the stable of Mobilia Gallery, the highly respected crafts gallery in Cambridge, Massachusetts, known for exhibiting quality Studio Jewelry. In addition to solo shows that enabled MacNeil to present bodies of work rarely seen in their entirety,[32] gallerists Libby and JoAnne Cooper have regularly included her in their frequent, theme-based survey exhibitions. Interestingly, even today, after more than twenty years of exhibiting her work, they note that many new clients still choose MacNeil's jewelry, not because of her reputation but because of its wearability and her skill with glass.[33]

In the 1990s, galleries such as Susan Cummins (Mill Valley, California), Facèré (Seattle), and Jewelers'Werk (Washington, DC) were building respected stables of contemporary jewelers; however, those involved in glass—even William Warmus with his short-lived Jewelry Project[34]—responded best to MacNeil's work because their clients were familiar with the contemporary glass market and thus had a context within which to understand MacNeil's prices.[35] Today, the dealers in contemporary glass who have shown MacNeil's work recall that while they were always very interested in it, they focused their efforts on promoting glass sculpture. They all note that MacNeil was one of very few Americans at that time regularly employing glass in jewelry whose works were on the level of the sculptors in their stables. Glass jewelry generally was purchased by women who, with their spouses, saw it as a way to complement their major purchases and patronage of contemporary glass sculptors. Many of these collectors still associated jewelry with precious materials. Recognizing these challenges, the galleries intentionally exhibited MacNeil in one-person shows paralleling those of Dailey.[36]

Since the opening on Madison Avenue in 1990 of Leo Kaplan Modern, a gallery for contemporary glass and furniture, which became the Scott Jacobson Gallery in 2009, dealer Jacobson was the most aggressive in marketing MacNeil's work, bringing it to such art fairs as SOFA Chicago, New York, and Santa Fe as they developed from 1994 to 2010 and to Wheaton Village's *GlassWeekends* in Millville, New Jersey. He advertised in *American Craft* magazine and even hired a contemporary jewelry and glass collector to help with sales. However, Jacobson maintained from the outset that he could never offer MacNeil a solo jewelry show because the market favored nonfunctional sculpture. Instead, he made it a practice from the early 1990s until 2008 to always feature MacNeil's jewelry alongside Dailey's annual sculpture exhibitions. Since his focus was not contemporary jewelry, he marketed her work as "wearable sculpture."[37]

Proactive in temperament, MacNeil began the highly popular but controversial "Mesh" series in 1995 and continued to develop it through 2004, then resumed it in 2008. This less complex, and, therefore, less expensive, line adds a late twentieth-century twist to the popular Renaissance style of pendants suspended from chains.[38] Returning to her 1979 *Necklace and Bracelet* (Plate 1 A–B), MacNeil substituted for the handcrafted woven metal a commercial rolled-brass screening—feeling that it provided a more contemporary look—that was then gold-plated. The commercial product was available in various diameters, which enabled her to vary the sizes of the pendants. To her surprise, the chains themselves had such physical presence that some collectors wanted to purchase only them; yet, for her, the pendants are the focal point of these compositions (see Plate 30). Their bold, minimal language rendered in strong color resulted in compelling, abstract graphic imagery. Once the pâte de verre production facilities in the studio were complete, MacNeil adopted it along with polished and/or acid-polished plate glass, Vitrolite, and optical glass as her vocabulary. Fabricated from the Daum scrap glass, the pâte de verre added a soft, almost voluptuous quality to the geometric compositions. In its utter simplicity, *Necklace No. 54* from 1997 (Figure 6), with its gently swelling, centrally placed circular form bursting from the rectilinear background, is one of the series' most lyrical works.

During the first five years of the "Mesh" series, MacNeil also started several other bodies of work: the "Ram's Horn Necklaces" series (1995–2003) (see Plate 21), the "Ram's Horn Mesh" series (1997–2003), the "Tri Ram's Horn Mesh" series (1997–2005), the "Lotus" series (1999–2000), the "Nexus" series (1999–2010), and the "Snowflake" series (1999). In addition, looking for an alternate form that required less effort in achieving wearability, she began to make brooches. On one level, what unites many of these series is the repetition of increasingly identifiable, organic motifs, such as the stylized lotus flower (see Plates 26 and 27) or the ram's head (see Plate 20), which demonstrates her interest in Ancient Egyp-

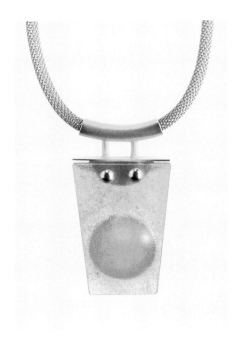

6 Linda MacNeil. *Necklace No. 54* from the "Mesh" series, 1997 (detail of Plate 19).

7 Linda MacNeil. *Fan Fair Necklace*, "Nexus" series, no. 13, 2001 (detail of Plate 25).

tian art. In 1998, MacNeil acquired a reprint of a study commissioned by Napoleon Bonaparte during his 1798–1801 Egyptian campaign that visually documents motifs on ancient monuments.[39] It became a source book for ornamental details that MacNeil would use for the next decade.

These six series advanced MacNeil's investigation of glass within a jewelry context. Her sophisticated arrangements address glass as a substitute for precious stones as well as such formal dichotomies as transparency versus opacity, mass versus void, "floating/supporting, linked/separate."[40] Metal-casting was the foundation. Each series has its own particular vocabulary of cast forms, with some overlap in the "Ram's Horn Necklaces" and the "Ram's Horn Mesh" series.

Two works from the "Nexus" series, *Fan Fair Necklace*, 2001, and *Blue Water Necklace*, 2010, completed within a nine-year span, demonstrate the complexity of MacNeil's compositions. Their structures are similar: small, cast-metal forms that contain shaped polished or acid-polished glass are hinged to openwork chains. The results differ because of the treatment of the glass: *Fan Fair Necklace* (Plate 25) is a sporty piece with funky, pillowlike glass cubes topped by custom-made screws attached to intricate openwork (Figure 7); *Blue Water Necklace* (Plate 43), on the other hand, is a very formal statement, addressing luminosity and transparency using shades of polished blue plate glass in descending intensity. The alternating deep blue plate-glass forms and clear glass prisms that comprise its attached pendant are hinged to move with the wearer's body (Figure 8).

MacNeil's residency at Ireland's Waterford Crystal Ltd in 1999 was, in a sense, one of the crowning points of her career, although she chose not to work in Waterford's characteristic faceted, hard-edged aesthetic. She went as part of a

8 Linda MacNeil. *Blue Water Necklace*, "Nexus" series, no. 22, 2010 (detail of Plate 43).

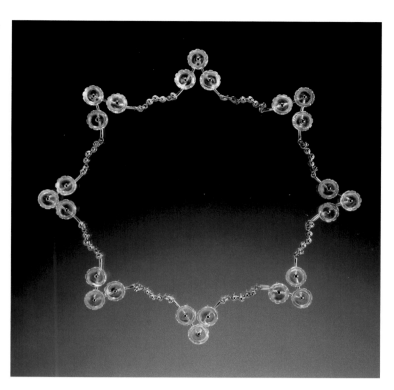

9 Linda MacNeil. *Snowflake Necklace No. 1*, 1999. Lead crystal and 18k yellow gold. 15 1/4 x 1 1/8 x 3/8 inches (38.7 x 2.9 x 1.0 cm) (open).
Collection of Joan and Jay Ochroch. Photo © Bill Truslow Photography.

10 Linda MacNeil. *Lotus Necklace No. 6*, 2000 (detail of Plate 23).

program established a year earlier to encourage dialogue between Studio Glass artists and Waterford workers. Dailey and three other artists initially went in 1998; MacNeil joined Dailey on his second trip in the winter of 1999. Given unlimited access to the factory's crystal and resources, MacNeil was specifically asked to work with the engravers. She focused her efforts on three bodies of work: the "Lotus," "Ram's Horn," and "Snowflake" (Figure 9) series. She fabricated the metal components and conceptualized the glass designs before leaving for Waterford and assembled them upon her return.

MacNeil remembers with pleasure having the equipment and employees at the factory available for two weeks. Master engraver Eamonn Hartley (Ireland, born 1957) added facial features to several of her hand-sculpted "Ram's Horn" heads (see Plate 33). She is most proud, however, of the crystal contours for the "Lotus" necklaces (see Figure 10), which Dailey and Richard Royal (United States, born 1952), another artist-in-residence who often blows components for Dailey's sculptures, started on their own at the factory.[41] After MacNeil cold-worked them, the Waterford cutters cut MacNeil's linear motif on the verso. *Lotus Necklace No. 6* (Plate 23) is a masterful example of her resolution of issues of linkage and materiality that concerned her at the time.

LOOKING BACK AND FORWARD
(2001 ONWARD)

In 2002, the first book of MacNeil's jewelry, *United in Beauty: The Jewelry and Collectors of Linda MacNeil*, was published. Containing an introductory essay by Helen W. Drutt English and an in-depth text by Suzanne Ramljak, writer, curator, and editor of several noted art periodicals including *Metalsmith* magazine, it "celebrated" MacNeil's patrons. The book was initially intended to complement a retrospective exhibition that Ramljak was organizing for the Mint Museum of Craft + Design in Charlotte, North Carolina, but scheduling problems caused the book to premiere independently.

The publication was intended to "reveal the character of individuals who have chosen to make a personal statement and adorn themselves with one of a kind works of art."[42] Aware of some European jewelers' decisions to illustrate their works on the body, MacNeil decided to have the jewelry worn by collectors.[43] Photography sessions were organized at seven locations around the country. The effort culminated at SOFA Chicago 2002 with a book signing at Leo Kaplan Modern's booth; attendees wore MacNeil necklaces.

Sculptural Radiance: The Jewelry and Objects of Linda MacNeil, the artist's 2003 solo exhibition at the Mint Museum of Craft + Design, was critically well received.[44] Consisting of approximately fifty works selected from various phases of MacNeil's career, it culminated with the new "Florals," which continue today. MacNeil considers "Florals" a radical departure from previous work, recently noting, "I made a decision to change. Some of my patrons were not interested in strict geometry. Nature with its organic shapes is the ultimate design master." The series started as pendants with attached chains; MacNeil then reverted to the strung bead format of the "Elements" necklaces for the "Bouquet" necklaces,

11 Linda MacNeil. *Amber Glow*, "Floral" series,
no. 16, 2001–2002 (detail of Plate 26).

12 Linda MacNeil. *Egyptian Reed Necklace*,
"Floral" series, no. 36, 2003 (detail of Plate 28).

at times adding a monumental pendant, as in *Primavera Necklace* (Plate 41). Concurrently, beginning in 2007, she developed a sequence of brooches (see Plates 37, 46, and 47) that were the subject of a 2013 exhibition at Mobilia Gallery in Cambridge, Massachusetts.

The "Florals" actually appear to be a logical progression from the "Mesh" necklaces and MacNeil's other series at the end of the century. Some chains consist of cast metal elements (see Plate 26); others, such as the elegant, curvilinear one of *Luxuriant Blossom Necklace* (Plate 36), are hand-manipulated stock. Shaped glass forms, such as those in *Amber Glow* (Figure 11), recall those of the "Mesh" series: they are simple, bold, and organic. Their imagery, however, is more realistic, evoking plant life or Ancient Egyptian scarabs. Some glass forms (Figure 12) bear patterns resembling hieroglyphics, which are stenciled and then sandblasted on their surfaces—a stylistic development perhaps resulting from Mac-Neil's research into carved gems in museum collections at the time.

Most remarkable in the "Florals" series is the strong color. Empowered by her success with pâte de verre, MacNeil recalled "aching" at the time for ways to expand her palette. While working concurrently on *Neckpiece No. 40* from the "Elements" series (Plate 31), she found the solution in stained-glass sample sets: she laminated their sheets of colored glass between layers of clear plate glass and mirrors.

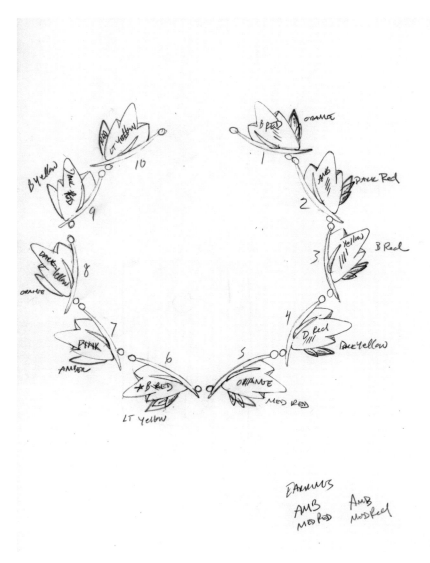

13 Linda MacNeil. Working drawing, *Bouquet Necklace* from the "Floral" series, ca. 2007. Photocopy with pencil. 11 1/2 x 8 inches (29.2 x 20.3 cm). Collection of the Linda MacNeil Archives, New Hampshire. Photo © Bill Truslow Photography.

While the first "Florals" were equally about metal and glass, the "Bouquets," a subset of the "Floral Necklaces" begun in 2005, present MacNeil's color sensibility at its best. All "Bouquet" necklaces (see Plate 34) have the word "Bouquet" as part of their titles. They use the same interconnected cast 18k yellow gold components as their substructure; the permutations of colored glass "flowers" are their defining trait. Interestingly, often the working drawings for both the "Bouquets" (see Figure 13) and some of the "floral" brooches featured in Mobilia Gallery's 2013 exhibition (see Plate 38 A–D) include potential color arrangements alongside detailed drawings of the composition, her standard practice in realizing a design (see Plate 40).[45]

Two commissions around the middle of the first decade of the millennium led MacNeil to explore "classic traditions in jewelry."[46] For her, that meant intro-

14 Linda MacNeil. *Primavera Necklace*, "Floral" series, no. 98, 2008–16 (detail of Plate 41).

ducing diamonds into her compositions. Klara Silverstein's request for a "Floral" necklace with pavé-set diamonds and platinum was followed by a request from the renowned collector and supporter of contemporary crafts Mrs. Nanette L. Laitman for an ensemble: a necklace, earrings, and ring that juxtaposed diamonds in significant quantities with the glass. Familiar with both the jewelry of Surrealist Salvador Dalí (Spain, 1904–1989) and Lalique's treatment of diamonds and glass in jewelry, MacNeil was excited by the projects. Lacking experience in setting stones or using platinum, she turned to specialty jewelers, including, through the years, Gary Roe (United States, born 1966) and Kent Raible (United States, born 1955).[47] In addition to setting stones, these craftsmen have provided other services, such as fabricating high-quality gold castings based upon MacNeil's molds, laser welding (a substitute for soldering), and granulation (fusing at one point of contact preformed grains often of gold or silver to a solid metal surface), enabling the artist to maintain the perfection in craftsmanship that characterizes her work.

In MacNeil's design for *Sparkling Water Necklace* (Plate 29), discrete pavé-set diamonds accent the pâte de verre and plate-glass forms. Laitman's *Necklace No. 41* (Plate 32) was a more difficult challenge because the patron did not want the precious stones to overwhelm the artist's established aesthetic.[48] MacNeil used *Necklace No. 1* (Plate 18) from the "Mirrored Glass" series as inspiration for the cut and polished plate-glass forms of *Necklace No. 41*; their pyramidal shape suggests large diamonds. The forms are attached to two polished parallel collars of 18k white gold set with a row of small diamonds. MacNeil's complex hinges enable the forms to move with the body. This signature work represented

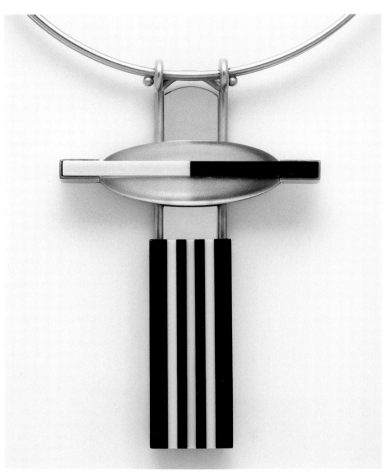

15 Linda MacNeil. *Necklace No. 117* from the "Mesh" series, 2008–2009 (detail of Plate 42).

16 Linda MacNeil. *Collar No. 18* from the "Neck Collar" series, 2010 (detail of Plate 45).

MacNeil's aesthetic in the noteworthy 2007 traveling exhibition *GlassWear*, curated for New York's Museum of Arts & Design and for the Schmuckmuseum Pforzheim in Germany by Ursula Ilse-Neuman, Cornelie Holzach, and Jutta-Annette Page. The exhibition documented, for the first time, the trend among contemporary international jewelry artists to incorporate glass in their oeuvre.[49]

MacNeil went on to introduce diamonds into other series. In some "Lucent Lines" necklaces from 2008, diamonds serve to underscore the highly geometric, formal qualities of the glass pendants and their chains (see Plate 39). *Primavera Necklace* (Plate 41), her most recently completed work from the "Floral" series, is perhaps her grandest homage to date to Lalique; here, in a manner reminiscent of the master, strips of set diamonds are juxtaposed with the acid-polished, mirrored glass, enhancing its luminosity (Figure 14). Perhaps most intriguing, however, is a very small group of brooches and pendants for the "Mesh" series completed between 2005 and 2013 that are thematically linked by a small, central, rectilinear form cut into the plate glass and outlined with diamonds, a motif inspired by House of Mauboussin designs. *Necklace No. 117* is particularly noteworthy because of the stark contrast between the central, geometric form outlined in diamonds and the surrounding undulating decorative patterns in the glass (Figure 15).

Over the past decade, MacNeil has continued to revisit earlier series. Her most dramatic revision is to the "Neck Collars." After seeing them together at the Mint Museum of Craft + Design's mid-career survey, she reworked the form as monumental pendants emphasizing color, geometry, and surface decoration (see Figure 16) that hang from simple 24k gold–plated brass collars (see Plate 48). Completed between 2010 and 2013, these statements are to date the most powerful "wearable sculptures"[50] of MacNeil's career. Moreover, they can be worn with casual clothes.[51]

In 2011, MacNeil was invited to join the American Jewelry Design Council (AJDC), a small, elite organization of Studio Jewelers and metalsmiths running large studios with multiple employees. Its mission is to further the education and promotion of excellence in jewelry design.[52] Mindful of the marketplace, its members create consummately crafted, beautiful, wearable jewelry, often with the most exquisite materials. MacNeil believes she has finally found her niche: "My experience as a member has been very fulfilling because of the sharing of career stories, techniques, and good old friendships. I respect every member because each one of them is a consummate professional and we openly share technical information and business methods for jewelers."

The parameters of art jewelry continue to evolve and be defined; history will determine how MacNeil's role is perceived. During the past few years, her work has continued to be shown in such Studio Glass exhibitions as *Studio Glass: Anna and Joe Mendel Collection* (The Montreal Museum of Fine Arts, 2010) and, more recently, *Glass Today: 21st-Century Innovations* (Museum of American Art, New Britain, Connecticut, 2014). However, she also has begun to be featured in exhibitions of major contemporary jewelry collections, such as that of Daphne Farago.[53] Without doubt, MacNeil has inserted her own distinctive interpretation into recent discourses on beauty and the nature of adornment. The central question—are her works "wearable [glass] sculpture"[54] or "new [jewelry] classics"?[55]—is still a subject for debate.

Author's note: Unless otherwise indicated, all information about the artist and quotations by the artist are drawn from a series of personal communications between the artist and the author. The conversations were held between January 19 and 23, 2015, and October 20, 2015 and January 10, 2016; the emails span January 2015 through January 2016.

1   Sharon Church, personal communication with the author, August 28, 2015; Susan Cummins, personal communications with the author, August 28 and 31, 2015. A relatively new term, "art jewelry" is defined as work that serves as a vehicle for contemporary expression and does not function solely in a supportive role in its relationship to the body. For a general discussion of the term, see Liesbeth den Besten, *On Jewellery: A Compendium of International Contemporary Art Jewellery* (Stuttgart: Arnoldsche Art Publishers, 2011), pp. 9–10.

2   Jane Friedman, "Kindred Spirits," *AmericanStyle*, Summer 2002, p. 73; see also Liz Eddins, "Marriage of the Minds," *Views: Rhode Island School of Design*, Fall 2000, pp. 14–15.

3   Dan Dailey, personal communication with the author, July 19, 2015.

4   For discussions of the influence of Erling Heistad and the Haystack-Hinckley School of Crafts, see Erling Heistad, personal communication with the author, August 29, 2015; Erling Heistad, email to Linda MacNeil, August 31, 2015. See also Elizabeth Dziadik, "Heistad Keeps Dartmouth's Best-Kept Secret Running Smoothly," November 15, 1996, at http://thedartmouth.com/1996/11/15/heistad-keeps-dartmouths-best-kept-secret-running-smoothly/.

5   Linda MacNeil, email to Erling Heistad, August 31, 2015.

6   See J. Fred Woell, "Linda MacNeil: New Work, David Bernstein Gallery, Boston, MA," *Metalsmith* 3, 4 (Fall 1983), p. 47.

7 For discussions of the evolution of MacNeil's aesthetic, see Suzanne Ramljak, "United in Beauty: The Jewelry and Collectors of Linda MacNeil," in Suzanne Ramljak and Helen W. Drutt English, *United in Beauty: The Jewelry and Collectors of Linda MacNeil* (Atglen, Pennsylvania: Schiffer Publishing, Ltd., 2002), pp. 17–25, passim; "Linda MacNeil: Jewelry & Objects," Suzanne Ramljak Folder, Linda MacNeil Archives, New Hampshire (hereafter: MacNeil Archives); Mint Museum of Craft + Design News Release: "Sculptural Radiance: The Jewelry and Objects of Linda MacNeil, August 9–November 23, 2003," Linda MacNeil Artist File, American Craft Council Library, Minneapolis.

8 See Eleni Cocordas, "Linda MacNeil: Helen Drutt Gallery, Philadelphia, Pa.," *Metalsmith* 9, 1 (Winter 1989), p. 48.

9 Linda MacNeil, "Glass Elements Series Description," unnamed file, MacNeil Archives.

10 Dailey has always acid-polished MacNeil's work for her. Initially, it was done in their studio, but Dailey now does both his own work and MacNeil's in a factory in West Virginia.

11 See Arline Fisch, *Textile Techniques in Metal* (New York: Van Nostrand Reinhold, 1975).

12 Libby Cooper, personal communication with the author, June 30, 2015.

13 The early hand mirrors were wall-hung to focus attention on their patterned handles. See Karen S. Chambers, "Linda MacNeil: A Detailed Look," *Metalsmith* 16, 3 (Summer 1996), pp. 27, 31.

14 MacNeil's first one-person show in New York was at Julie: Artisans' Gallery located on Madison Avenue, which was developing its reputation as a center for wearable art.

15 The hand mirror featured in the 1980 *New Glass Review* was chosen by the then Corning Museum of Glass director Thomas S. Buechner, assistant curator of twentieth-century glass William Warmus, and J. Stewart Johnson, Department of Architecture and Design, The Museum of Modern Art, New York. The fourth juror, Dan Dailey, abstained from commenting upon MacNeil's work. See William Warmus, "Introduction," in *New Glass Review* (Corning, New York: The Corning Museum of Glass, 1980), p. 9.

16 See "Portfolio: Linda MacNeil," *American Craft* 40, 1 (February–March 1980), p. 45.

17 Dailey introduced MacNeil to many glass sculptors who would, over time, contribute significantly to the field and influence her aesthetic. Ben Tré taught her to cast glass while the three were at Pilchuck Glass School in Stanwood, Washington, in the late 1970s. In 1981, she became better acquainted with Libenský and Brychtová when Dailey, as president of the Glass Art Society, invited them to be guest speakers at its annual conference in Seattle. MacNeil had long admired their work after seeing it at the 1967 Montreal Exposition. Vízner was a close friend of Dailey and a frequent visitor. Howard Ben Tré, personal communication with the author, May 23, 2015.

18 Kate Dobbs Ariail, "Reviews: Sculptural Radiance: The Jewelry and Objects of Linda MacNeil, Mint Museum of Craft + Design, Charlotte, North Carolina, August 9–November 23, 2003," *Metalsmith* 24, 3 (Summer 2004), p. 48.

19 See Robert A. M. Stern, *The International Design Yearbook 1985/86* (New York: Abbeville Press, 1985), vol. 1, pp. 130–31.

20 They received mixed response when included in MacNeil's 2003 Mint Museum mid-career survey show. See Ariail, p. 48.

21 Scott Jacobson, personal communication with the author, August 4, 2015.

22 See Terri Lonier, "Linda MacNeil: Artistic Innovation in Glass," *Neues Glas* 2 (1985), cover, pp. 60–66.

23 See Linda MacNeil, postcard to Dan Klein, June 19, 1987, MacNeil Archives.

24 Linda MacNeil, "Neck Collar Series Description," Linda McNeil Interview Questions Folder, MacNeil Archives.

25 Ibid.

26 Cocordas, p. 48.

27 Ibid.; Bonnie J. Miller, "A Matter of Scale: Innovations in American Glass Jewelry," *Glasswork* 15 (July 1993), p. 22.

28 Laurie Stein, "In Search of History: The Evolution and Patronage of Contemporary Metalwork and Jewelry," in Davira S. Taragin, ed.,*Contemporary Crafts and the Saxe Collection* (Toledo, Ohio, and New York: The Toledo Museum of Art and Hudson Hills Press, 1993), p. 172.

29 Helen W. Drutt English, personal communication with the author, August 4, 2015.

30 Linda MacNeil, letter to Susan Lewin, May 5, 1989, unnamed folder, MacNeil Archives.

31 Anna Mendel, personal communications with the author, September 8 and 9, 2015.

32 In 2013, for example, Mobilia Gallery gave MacNeil a one-person exhibition of brooches completed between 2000 and 2013.

33 Cooper.

34 With the increasing popularity of Studio Glass among collectors in the 1990s, William Warmus joined with the collector Sheri Sandler in 1993 to promote glass jewelry as part of larger developments in the medium. Calling their endeavor The Jewelry Project, that year they showed MacNeil's work as well as jewelry by such artists as Julie Mihalisin alongside the small glass sculptures of Tom Patti and Paul Stankard at art fairs like Wheaton Village's *GlassWeekend* in Millville, New Jersey, and *Chicago International New Art Forms Exposition*, the predecessor to SOFA Chicago. William Warmus, personal communication with the author, August 25, 2015. See also "The Jewelry Project," *Chicago International New Art Forms Exposition 1993* (Chicago: The Lakeside Group, 1993), p. 96; Wheaton Village, Millville, New Jersey, "The Glass Jewel: An Exhibition of The Jewelry Project," *GlassWeekend '93: A Symposium & Exhibition of Contemporary Glass* (organized by the Art Alliance for Contemporary Glass, The Corning Museum of Glass, and The Creative Glass Center of America) (Millville, New Jersey: Wheaton Village, 1993), p. 36.

35 Cummins.

36 Lynn Leff, personal communication with the author, August 26, 2015; Tom Riley, personal communication with the author, September 16, 2015; Lindsey Scott, personal communications with the author, August 5 and September 16 and 17, 2015. For a general discussion of MacNeil's collectors, see Ramljak, *United in Beauty*, pp. 28–30.

37 Scott Jacobson, personal communications with the author, May 16 and August 4, 2015; Leff.

38 Chambers, p. 33.

39 See *Description de L'Egypte Publiée par les orders de Napoléon Bonaparte*," text by Gilles Néret (Cologne: Benedikt Taschen, 1994), passim.

40 Ariail, p. 48.

41 Tina Oldknow with artist's biography by Margery Aronson, *Linda MacNeil: Original and Unique Works in Waterford Crystal* (Kilbarry, Waterford, Ireland: Waterford Wedgwood, PLC, n.d.), passim.

42 "Linda MacNeil Jewelry," Linda MacNeil Looseleaf, MacNeil Archives.

43 Joe [Rapone], letter to Linda MacNeil, October 8, 1999, Mobilia Gallery Folder, MacNeil Archives; Cooper.

44 See Ariail, p. 48; Joan Falconer Byrd, "Review: Linda MacNeil/Mint Museum of Craft + Design, Charlotte, NC, August 9–November 23, 2003," *American Craft* 64, 1 (February–March 2004), pp. 78–79.

45 When MacNeil decides to realize a particular design, she carefully draws all the details for one half of the composition if the other half is a mirror image.

46 "Linda MacNeil: Artist Statement," March 2010; "Constellations," n.d., MacNeil Archives.

47 Both MacNeil and Raible were represented in the critically acclaimed 2003 exhibition *The Art of Gold*, organized by the Society of North American Goldsmiths.

48 Mrs. Nanette L. Laitman, personal communication with the author, December 3, 2015.

49 See Ursula Ilse-Neuman, Cornelie Holzach, and Jutta-Annette Page, *GlassWear: Glass in Contemporary Jewelry* (Stuttgart: Arnoldsche Art Publishers in collaboration with the Museum of Arts & Design, New York, and the Schmuckmuseum Pforzheim, Pforzheim, Germany, 2007), pp. 138–39.

50 Colleen and John Kotelly, personal communication with the author, October 18, 2015.

51 Jacobson, August 4, 2015.

52 See George Sawyer, "The Collection," in *Variations on a Theme: 25 Years of Designs from the AJDC* (Hermitage, Pennsylvania: American Jewelry Design Council, 2014), pp. 8–9.

53 One of MacNeil's early "Neck Collars" was included in the Asheville (North Carolina) Art Museum exhibition *Flourish: Selected Jewelry from the Daphne Farago Collection*, April 18–August 16, 2015.

54 Jacobson, August 4, 2015.

55 See *New Glass Review 17* (Corning, New York: The Corning Museum of Glass, 1996), p. 75.

UNMISTAKABLY MACNEIL

Ursula Ilse-Neuman

As a leading figure in contemporary art jewelry, Linda MacNeil has broken new ground, drawing upon centuries, if not millennia, of jewelry history while absorbing current trends in the fine arts, architecture, and design. Mining and reinterpreting historical styles and transforming them with her new and unique perspective, MacNeil personifies the postmodernist sensibility.[1] The freedom either to accept or defy conventions is inherent in her approach to jewelry design and fabrication.

The distinguishing characteristics of MacNeil's jewelry are its predominantly nonobjective aesthetic and its masterful integration of glass and metal into refined compositions that balance line, color, and light. So, too, the concerns of the wearer are essential design considerations for MacNeil. Her necklaces and brooches are meant to be worn and are complete only when they complement and enhance the body.

The origins of the highly diverse and vigorous American art jewelry scene in which MacNeil has earned her reputation lie in the Studio Jewelry movement, part of the broader Studio Craft movement that also included furniture, textiles, ceramics, glass, and metalwork. This movement began in earnest in America at the end of World War II and had fully flowered by the 1970s.[2]

Arguably, the greatest influence upon American Studio Jewelry can be traced not to a jeweler but to a sculptor, Alexander Calder (United States, 1898–1976), who fabricated jewelry for his family and friends by using simple, intuitive processes and nontraditional materials, including brass, steel wire, ceramics, wood, and found glass. Calder's sculptural jewelry demonstrated that value could be derived from artistic content rather than precious materials—a tenet that continues to exert a major influence on American art jewelry to this day.

Whereas Calder was an artist who made jewelry as a diversion, a group of jewelers in the 1930s and 1940s made it their goal to create jewelry that was art. Located in New York's Greenwich Village, the epicenter of the art world at the time,[3] these avant-garde jewelers, most of them self-taught, began fashioning modernist jewelry inspired by twentieth-century art movements, including Cubism, Dadaism, Surrealism, Constructivism, and Abstract Expressionism.

Around the same time, on the West Coast, Margaret De Patta (United States, 1903–1964) adopted the Constructivist ideas of former Bauhaus master László Moholy-Nagy (Hungary, 1895–1946) after attending his School of Design in Chicago in 1940. With little formal jewelry-making training, she worked with a lapidary to create dazzling visual effects by using quartz crystals to integrate light, space, and structure into her modernist jewelry (see Figure 1).[4]

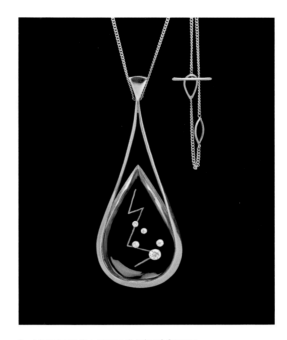

1 Margaret De Patta (United States, 1903–1964). *Pendant*, 1960. White gold, quartz, and diamonds 3 x 2 ½ x ⅜ inches (7.6 x 6.4 x 1 cm) (without chain).
Collection of the Museum of Arts and Design, New York, gift of Eugene Bielawski, The Margaret De Patta Bequest, through the American Craft Council, 1976. Photo by John Bigelow Taylor, 2008.

The Studio Jewelry movement gained momentum following World War II, when a sizable group of returning veterans entered craft programs under the GI Bill, only to discover that training opportunities for metalworkers and jewelers were extremely limited.[5] Responding to their need, the noted silversmith and jeweler Margret Craver (United States, 1907–2010) took the initiative and organized a series of workshops that were instrumental in leading America's metalsmiths from the traditionalist constraints of the early twentieth century into the individualism of the mid-twentieth century. Held between 1947 and 1951 at the Rhode Island School of Design (RISD) in Providence and the Rochester Institute of Technology in Rochester, New York, and led by some of the finest British and European silversmiths, these workshops produced a new generation of well-trained American jewelers who were also dedicated to teaching and changing the very nature of their craft.[6]

The postwar establishment and expansion of jewelry-making courses within the more encompassing intellectual setting of college and university campuses opened avenues of humanist inquiry that encouraged individualism and experimentation beyond the mere mastery of jewelry techniques.[7] Jewelry was becoming appreciated as art, and craftsmen as artists, a development observed by the jeweler and metal sculptor Albert Paley (United States, born 1944): "Prior to the '60s, craftsmen were makers, artists were thinkers. I tried to bring craft to the level of art by giving it more of an intellectual context. I resented the image of a humble craftsman."[8]

2 J. Fred Woell (United States, 1934–2015). *The Good Guys,* 1966. Walnut, steel, copper, plastic, silver, and gold leaf. 4 x 4½ x ½ inches (10.2 x 11.4 x 1.3 cm). Collection of the Museum of Arts and Design, New York, gift of the Johnson Wax Company, through the American Craft Council, 1977. Photo by John Bigelow Taylor, 2008.

By the 1960s, the pioneering Studio jewelers of the 1940s and 1950s had been actively working for more than twenty years and were at the height of their artistic powers. They were joined by up-and-coming American jewelers whose solid technical foundation produced sophisticated work that began to attract considerable attention in the larger craft and art world in galleries and museum exhibitions.

When Linda MacNeil attended three of America's leading jewelry programs in the 1970s, she was introduced to the great diversity of approaches and techniques that jewelry artists were exploring. She used the opportunity to learn new fabrication methods, even though the styles and intent of much of the work she observed diverged from her own developing preferences. Through J. Fred Woell (United States, 1934–2015), her first jewelry teacher at the Haystack-Hinckley School of Crafts in Hinckley, Maine, and later at the Philadelphia College of Art, she witnessed the use of narrative content (see Figure 2) as the modernist idioms of the 1940s and 1950s were replaced with bold and often controversial social and political statements in response to the turbulent and dramatic events of the 1960s and 1970s: John F. Kennedy's assassination, the Civil Rights Movement, the Vietnam War, terrorism at the Munich Olympics, and Watergate. To incorporate this narrative content, artists commonly de-emphasized virtuoso metalworking techniques and used found objects and assemblage methods to create what effectively became small canvases that would carry their viewpoints into the world. The processes they used were not aligned with MacNeil's more formal and structural approach, nor was creating jewelry that carried strong political or social messages what she sought for herself.

Artists whose abstract works focused on materials and techniques were more in line with MacNeil's thinking, and, in that regard, the 1970s offered her plenty of food for thought. She acknowledges the influences of Stanley Lechtzin (United States, born 1936), whose reinvention of the nineteenth-century electro-forming process allowed him to make large, fantastic brooches and neck collars; Arline Fisch (United States, born 1931), whose application of intricate textile weaving and knitting techniques to metal created decorative and body-flattering wearable ornaments; Paley, whose dramatic, forged metalwork produced baroque sculptural pendants and brooches; and Marjorie Schick (United States, born 1941), whose boldly painted wooden brooches, referred to as "drawings to wear," as well as her outsized collars and bracelets, affirmed jewelry's role as sculpture and art.[9]

At this relatively early stage in her development, MacNeil had already begun to see a clear path amidst the polyphony of styles and ideas that surrounded her. She began expressing herself as a metalsmith and jeweler, taking a craftsmanly, decorative approach to creating jewelry intended to harmonize with and enhance the appearance of the wearer—jewelry that might be viewed as a reaction to the content-driven, perhaps less flattering, message-laden jewelry of the era.

The decisive event that established MacNeil's unique identity as a jewelry artist specializing in glass was her relationship with the renowned glass artist Dan Dailey (United States, born 1947), first as her teacher at the Massachusetts College of Art in Boston in 1974, where he introduced her to the glass medium, and then, two years later, as her life partner. By the 1970s, Studio Glass—to a greater extent than Studio Jewelry—had captured a knowledgeable and devoted following, and Dailey had branched off from the mainstream and achieved widespread recognition for unconventional yet elegant glass sculptures that incorporated metal and showcased his masterful glassmaking skills. Intrigued by glass's enormous potential for artistic expression, MacNeil widened her own focus and began working in the two media. On occasion over the years, they have made parts for each other's compositions, as in Dailey's *Rectangulaire*, from 1981 (Figure 3), for which MacNeil provided the metalwork.

During her studies at RISD between 1974 and 1976, MacNeil was immersed in a stimulating environment in which some of the most renowned glass artists and jewelers of the time interacted with students to challenge and expand their technical and artistic boundaries. She took an independent study class with the famed American glass artist Dale Chihuly (United States, born 1941) and was exposed to the latest approaches to glass and jewelry during her time at the school, primarily through John ("Jack") Prip (United States, 1922–2009), her primary teacher and critic at RISD. MacNeil continued steadfastly to perfect her own aesthetic even after she left RISD and acknowledges the influence that many renowned American and European jewelers have had on her development, including Max Fröhlich (Switzerland, 1908–1997), for his simplicity and craftsmanship; Claus Bury (Germany, born 1946), for his graphics and use of acrylics; Wendy Ramshaw (United Kingdom, born 1939), for her use of the lathe; David Watkins (United Kingdom, born 1940), for his design of rigid forms; Stanley Lechtzin, for the working mechanics of his neck collars; John Prip, for the ways to soften geometry; and Louis Mueller (United States, born 1943), for general design principles.[10]

3 Dan Dailey (United States, born 1947).
Rectangulaire from the "Tripod Vessels" series, 1981.
Blown glass, plate glass, Vitrolite glass, and 24k gold-plated brass. 11 5/8 x 8 1/2 x 8 1/2 inches
(29.5 x 21.6 x 21.6 cm).
Courtesy of the artist. Photo courtesy of the artist.

4 René Lalique (France, 1860–1945).
Carnation Brooch/Pendant, ca. 1901–1902. 18k gold, plique-à-jour enamel, glass, and baroque pearl.
3 x 2 x 1/2 inches (7.6 x 5.1 x 1.3 cm).
Collection of the Virginia Museum of Fine Arts, Richmond, gift of Sydney and Frances Lewis.
Photo by Travis Fullerton, © Virginia Museum of Fine Arts.

By focusing on glass as her principal jewelry component, Linda MacNeil added her name to a history that extends back more than five thousand years to man-made glass beads in Eastern Mesopotamia. This long history notwithstanding, with few exceptions, such as in Ancient Egypt, where glass was rare and valued as highly as precious stones or gold, or in Venice, where glass beads served for centuries as highly prized export articles, glass carried little value save for its ability to imitate gemstones. In fact, glass was often selected with the intention of deceiving the buyer—a practice attested to by the Roman scholar Pliny the Elder (AD 23–79), who warned his contemporaries to be on the alert for counterfeit gemstones made of glass.[11] In medieval Europe, the production and sale of imitation glass gemstones was strictly forbidden, with violations punishable by loss of the right hand and banishment. As glass-making technology advanced, new possibilities for subterfuge were presented, most prominently in the eighteenth-century French court of Louis XV, when the sparkle of paste glass with the addition of lead glass surpassed that of real diamonds.[12]

With such low standing as a material for exquisite jewelry, it is no wonder that MacNeil reveres the French glass designer and jeweler René Lalique (France,

5 Raymond Templier (France, 1891–1968). *Model for a Necklace*, date unknown. Graphite, gouache, and watercolor on paper. 6 1/8 x 7 1/4 inches (15.5 x 18.5 cm).

1860–1945) for putting glass center stage as an artistic medium in its own right. When MacNeil first visited the Musée des Beaux-Arts in Nancy, France, in the 1970s, she discovered its superb collection of Art Nouveau and Art Deco objects by Emile Gallé (France, 1846–1904) and the Daum studio (founded by Jean Daum, France, 1825–1885). In 1977, at the Musée des Arts Décoratifs in Paris, she found in Lalique a kindred spirit who shared her devotion to glass as a highly aesthetic and expressive material that offered her "the creative freedom to imagine and create forms that can be made with no other material."[13] This revelation, and her sojourn at the Daum factory, proved to be transformative and ultimately propelled MacNeil to national recognition as a master of the jewelry medium.[14]

MacNeil does not draw literally from Lalique in her work, but by combining and contrasting acid-polished and sand-blasted transparent glass with opaque Vitrolite glass, she achieves effects similar to those he was able to produce through his superlative use of pâte de verre by acid-polishing her glass surfaces. Her *Primavera Necklace* (Plate 41) recalls the spirit of the French master's love for nature and its organic forms (see Figure 4).

By the 1920s, Lalique and other jewelry makers were drawn to the new geometric shapes and straightened lines that proliferated after the 1925 Exposition Internationale in Paris.[15] This new modernist aesthetic, which came to be known as Art Deco, rose to prominence following the exposition and was heralded for its simplicity, elegance, comfort, and luxury. Although these four words apply aptly to the aesthetic spirit of MacNeil's work, her jewelry does not look backward to a society infatuated with jazz and the machine age but reinterprets the Art Deco style for today's cultural milieu. An example of one of MacNeil's Art Deco–inspired pieces is her *Neckpiece No. 41* from the "Elements" series (Plate 32). Although she did not use any specific Art Deco designs as models, such as the drawing in graphite, gouache, and watercolor by Raymond Templier (France, 1891–1968) (Figure 5), her interpretation maintains the elegant spirit of Art Deco luxury, albeit with a modern touch of irony, through her use of cut, polished, and mirrored glass "gemstones" as the main attraction, with diamonds relegated to bit players, thereby turning the hierarchy of preciousness on its head.

Art Deco jewelry design was heavily influenced by the revolutionary art of the early twentieth century, particularly Cubism, with its analytical vision of form and its re-examination of shapes through their abstraction and flattening. This can be observed in the work of Parisian jewelry designers Jean Fouquet (France, 1899–1994) and Jean Després (France, 1889–1980) (see Figures 6 and 7), both of whom used contrasting materials to accentuate overlapping geometric forms.[16] In her series of variegated neck collars (see Plates 44, 45, and 48), MacNeil achieved an even more reduced architectural unity by using fewer, although clearly delineated, balanced shapes and planes made of plate glass and Vitrolite framed by metal.

6   Jean Fouquet (France, 1899–1994). *Brooch*, 1925. White gold, yellow gold, onyx, lacquer, rock crystal, and brilliant-cut diamonds. 3 1/16 x 1/8 x 3/8 inches (7.8 x 6.2 x 1 cm). Collection of the Toledo Museum of Art, Toledo, Ohio, Mr. and Mrs. George M. Jones, Jr. Fund.

7   Jean Després (France, 1889–1980). *Pendant Brooch,* 1932. Silver, gold, onyx, and lacquer. 3 1/8 x 1 3/8 inches (8 x 3.5 cm). Collection of the Museé de l'Avallonnais, Avallon, France, gift of the artist. © Les Arts Décoratifs. Photo by Jean Tholance.

In addition to taking inspiration from unique pieces by bijoutiers-artistes such as Fouquet, Templier, and Després, MacNeil also examines the work of well-established French jewelry houses of the era out of regard for their engineering, which she sees as "the ultimate in art jewelry."[17] The use of diamonds in her *Necklace No. 117* (Plate 42) recalls the virtuoso diamond settings in a 1925 brooch by the famed Parisian firm of Mauboussin (Figure 8).[18]

Taking her studies of jewelry history even further back in time, MacNeil's oeuvre reflects her attraction to the rich materials, motifs, and style of the decorative objects of Ancient Egypt, an interest she credits to her visit to the 1976 *Treasures of Tutankhamun* exhibition at The Metropolitan Museum of Art, New York.[19] MacNeil's attraction echoes Art Deco's fascination with Egyptian art, which

8 Mauboussin. *Brooch,* ca. 1925.
Jadeite, moonstone, black onyx, diamonds, and platinum-plated 18k gold.
1³⁄₄ x 1³⁄₄ inches (4.5 x 4.5 cm).

9 *Falcon Pectoral of Tutankhamun,* Egypt,
Dynasty 18, ca. 1332–1323 BCE.
Carnelian, chalcedony, and glass paste.
2¹⁄₂ (H.) inches (6.5 cm).

had been inflamed by the sensational discovery of King Tut's tomb in 1922. The use of semiprecious stones in combination with glass and gold, as in Tutankhamun's spectacular pectoral (Figure 9), resonates strongly with her artistic sensibility.

In her elaborate *Lotus Necklace No. 2*, MacNeil focused on the ubiquitous Egyptian lotus motif (see Figure 10), juxtaposing the unique qualities of Waterford lead crystal with hot-worked glass and using 18k yellow gold to connect the abstracted lotus elements (Figure 11). In her *Egyptian Reed Necklace* (Plate 28), she stylized the lotus motif, refining the composition by contrasting the transparency and refraction of two kinds of glass—pâte de verre and acid-polished amber glass—and adding lines of gold-plated brass as bold elements of the design.

Of the many powerful images that have been transported into the Western decorative arts from Ancient Egypt, the ram's head as depicted in the superb gold amulet from ca. 712–664 BCE is iconic (Figure 12). In MacNeil's *Ram's Horn* (Plate 33), the image is reduced to its essential elements, retaining the innate energy and evocative symbolism of the original while creating a reductive form suitable for modern wearers.

MacNeil's inquisitiveness also extends to more recent accomplishments in the visual arts and design. *Hand Mirror No. 15* (Plate 3), part of a series of hand mirrors she created early in her career, while distinctly her own, demonstrates a clear relationship to the furniture, glass, and ceramic designs of the Milan-based Memphis group, which included the work of the American designer Peter Shire (born 1947) (see Figure 13).[20]

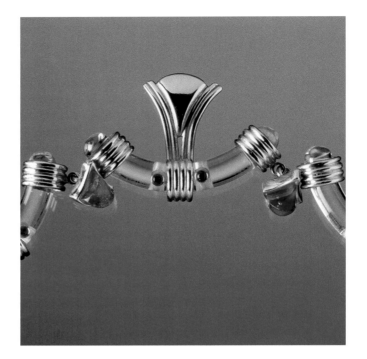

10 *Lotus Inlay,* Egypt, New
Kingdom, Dynasty 18,
ca. 1400–1300 BCE. Faience.
1 9/16 x 1 7/16 x 3/16 inches
(4 x 3.6 x 0.5 cm).
Collection of The Metropolitan
Museum of Art, New York. Photo
© The Metropolitan Museum of Art,
courtesy of Art Resource, NY.

11 Linda MacNeil. *Lotus Necklace No. 2,* 1999
(detail). Lead crystal, plate glass, hot-worked
glass, and 18k yellow gold. 6 1/2 x 6 1/2 x 1/4 inches
(16.5 x 16.5 x 0.6 cm).
Collection of the Currier Museum of Art, Manchester, New
Hampshire, purchased with funds from The Ed and Mary
Scheier Acquisition Fund.

Other MacNeil works that take cues from sources outside of jewelry history include her *Mondrian Brooch* (Figure 14); her *Necklace No. 4* (Plate 8), which suggests the gridlike structures of Minimalist artist Sol LeWitt; and her *Plate Glass Vessel No. 12* from 1984 (Plate 10), which may draw its inspiration from twentieth-century visions of utopian architecture. The contrasting colors of geometric abstraction are suggested in her *Neck Collar Ensemble No. 1* (Plate 12 A–C) while the sophisticated naiveté of cartoons infuses *Sublime* (Plate 37). These variations on modern and contemporary works of art are cast in her trademark combination of glass and metal, display her characteristic aesthetic, and exhibit her unwavering devotion to the decorative function of jewelry.

* * *

Since the 1970s, when MacNeil set out on her career, art jewelry has become increasingly "global," with ideas about design and fabrication traveling rapidly from one part of the world to another and from one culture to another. The debate concerning the use of precious versus nonprecious materials is by now irrelevant, as gold and gemstones commonly appear alongside less costly materials, a practice of combining the High and the Low[21] that MacNeil had adopted early in her career.

The desire to stand out in an increasingly crowded art jewelry field is often the driving force for emerging artists for whom nothing is taboo. MacNeil, by contrast, shuns superficial, "flashy" effects as her work continues to evolve and her curiosity and explorations steadily expand. Through impeccable craftsmanship and her sure eye for design, she has forged a strong cadre of devotees and has set a standard that has elevated the field and widened its appeal. Her elegant creations endure as objects of beauty and desire that are uniquely and unmistakably her own.

12 *Ram's Head Amulet,* Egypt and Sudan, possibly Nubia, Kushite period, Dynasty 25, ca. 712–664 BCE. Gold. 1⅝ x 1⁷⁄₁₆ x ¾ inches (4.2 x 3.6 x 2 cm).
Collection of The Metropolitan Museum of Art, New York, gift of Norbert Schimmel Trust, 1989. Photo © The Metropolitan Museum of Art, courtesy of Art Resource, NY.

13 Peter Shire (United States, born 1947). *Anchorage* teapot from the "Memphis" series, 1982. Nickel silver, lacquer, brass, and wood. 15¼ x 13 x 5¹³⁄₁₆ inches (38.7 x 33 x 14.7 cm).
Courtesy of Memphis, Milan. Photo by Studio Azzurro.

14 Linda MacNeil. *Mondrian Brooch,* "Brooch" series, no. 67, 2011. Plate glass, mirror, Vitrolite glass, and 24k gold-plated brass. 2¾ x 1 x ½ inches (7 x 2.5 x 1.3 cm).
Courtesy of the artist. Photo © Bill Truslow Photography.

1 The term "postmodernism" has been applied to movements in art, music, and literature that counter tendencies in modernism and are characterized through their revival of historical elements and techniques.

2 See Jeannine Falino, ed., *Crafting Modernism: Midcentury American Art and Design* (New York: Harry N. Abrams, 2011) for an explanation of the development of Studio Crafts.

3 Notable among them were Sam Kramer (1913–1964), Art Smith (1923–1982), Francisco Rebajes (1905–1990), and Ed Wiener (1918–1991).

4 MacNeil acknowledges the similarities of her work with De Patta's simple, clean, modern jewelry design. In an analogous fashion to De Patta's structural approach and innovative transformations of quartz into radiant gemstones, MacNeil plays with the effects of light and translucence using a wide range of colorful glass elements held in place by bright metalwork. Personal communication with the author, January 2016.

5 Ursula Ilse-Neuman, "A Community Emerges: The American Studio Jewelry Movement 1945–1960," in Falino, pp. 204–26.

6 The workshops were sponsored by the New York metal-refining company Handy and Harman. Attendees who would later become influential teachers included John Paul Miller (1918–2013), Earl Pardon (1926–1991), Alma Eikerman (1908–1995), Richard H. Reinhardt (1921–1998), and Carlyle Smith (1912–2004), who taught at Rhode Island School of Design, where his students included Robert Ebendorf (MA, 1963) and Richard Mawdsley (MA, 1969).

7 The schools included Rhode Island School of Design; Cranbrook Academy of Art, Bloomfield Hills, Michigan; Tyler School of Art in Philadelphia; State University of New York at New Paltz; and Massachusetts College of Art.

8 Deborah Norton, "A History of the School for American Craftsmen," *Metalsmith* 5, 1 (Winter 1985), p. 20.

9 Linda MacNeil, personal communication with the author, December 2015.

10 Ibid.

11 Pliny the Elder, *Natural History*, Book 37, pp. 242–43, 260–61.

12 See Jutta-Annette Page, "Glass As Jewels: An Uneasy Relationship," in Ursula Ilse-Neuman, Cornelie Holzach, and Jutta-Annette Page, *GlassWear: Glass in Contemporary Jewelry* (Stuttgart: Arnoldsche Art Publishers in collaboration with the Museum of Arts & Design, New York, and the Schmuckmuseum Pforzheim, Pforzheim, Germany, 2007) for the history of glass jewelry from its beginnings up to the early twentieth century.

13 Layla Khani, "Linda MacNeil Jewellery," *Visual Masters*, Winter 2011, p. 46, www.vmmag.co.uk.

14 In 2011, Linda MacNeil received the Master of the Medium award in the Metal/Jewelry category from the James Renwick Alliance.

15 Art Deco jewelry was strongly influenced by developments in the fine arts including Cubism, Futurism, and De Stijl.

16 In contrast to jewelry houses such as Cartier and Boucheron, Art Deco jewelers of the Union des Artistes Modernes, including Jean Després, Jean Fouquet, and Raymond Templier, emphasized craftsmanship over precious gemstones and advocated getting rid of excessive ornament.

17 MacNeil cites Mauboussin, Cartier, Fouquet, Lalique, and Van Cleef and Arpel as famous jewelry houses she enjoys looking at. Personal communication with the author, 2015.

18 The House of Mauboussin, founded in 1827, was awarded the Grand Prix at the 1925 *Exposition Internationale des Arts Décoratifs et Industriels Modernes* in Paris.

19 Linda MacNeil, personal communication with the author, January 2016.

20 The Memphis Group was formally founded by Ettore Sottsass in Milan in 1981.

21 The term was originated by Kirk Varnedoe for MOMA's 1990 exhibition *High And Low: Modern Art and Popular Culture*, which he co-curated with Adam Gopnik.

PLATES

PLATE 1 A–B *Necklace and Bracelet* from the "Elements" series, ca. 1979
Plate glass, sterling silver, and 14k yellow gold

(A) Necklace: 18 x ⁷⁄₈ x 1 inches (45.7 x 2.2 x 2.5 cm) (open)
(B) Bracelet: 8 ¹⁵⁄₁₆ x ³⁄₄ x ⁷⁄₈ inches (22.7 x 1.9 x 2.2 cm) (open)

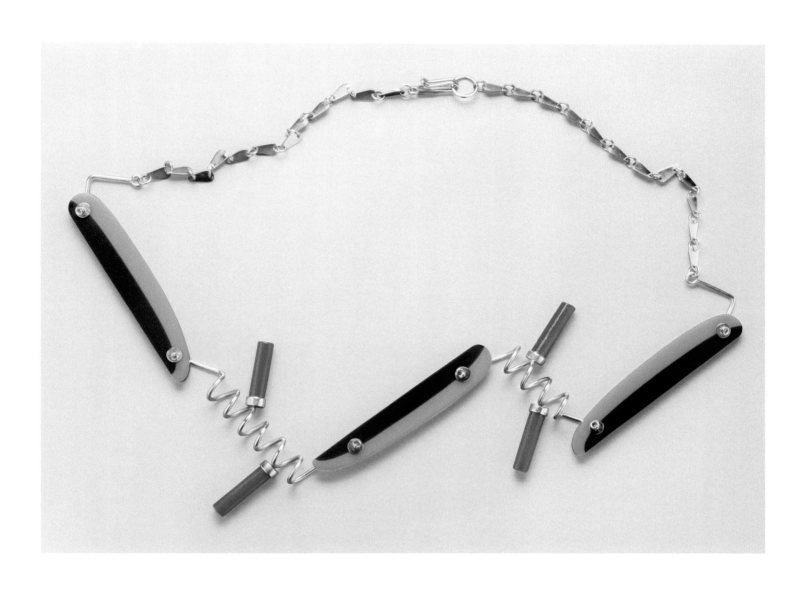

PLATE 2   *Neckpiece No. 2* from the "Elements" series, 1979
Vitrolite glass and 14k yellow gold. 19 $\frac{1}{2}$ x 2 $\frac{1}{4}$ x $\frac{3}{8}$ inches (49.53 x 5.7 x 1 cm) (open)

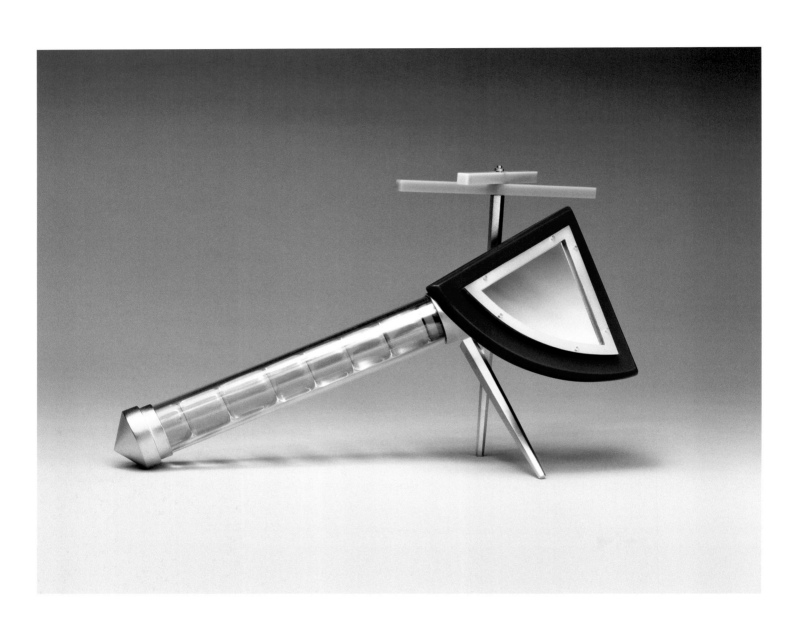

PLATE 3 *Hand Mirror No. 15*, 1979–81
Vitrolite glass, mirror, plate glass, found glass tubing, and 24k gold-plated brass. 8 x 12 x 4 inches (20.3 x 30.5 x 10.2 cm)

PLATE 4 *Hand Mirror No. 11,* 1980
Hot-worked glass, Vitrolite glass, and 24k gold–plated brass. 12 x 6 x 4 inches (30.5 x 15.2 x 10.2 cm)

PLATE 5 *Neckpiece No. 20* from the "Elements" series, 1982
Vitrolite glass, plate glass, and 14k yellow gold. 16 x 1 x ³⁄₈ inches (40.6 x 2.5 x 1 cm) (open)

PLATE 6 *Neckpiece No. 22* from the "Elements" series, 1983
Hot-worked glass, plate glass, and 14k yellow gold. 15 1/4 x 1 1/4 x 7/16 inches (38.7 x 3.2 x 1.1 cm) (open)

PLATE 7 *Necklace No. 3* from the "Lucent Lines" series, 1983
Plate glass and 14k yellow gold. $23\frac{1}{2}$ x 1 x $\frac{1}{4}$ inches (59.7 x 2.5 x 0.6 cm) (open)

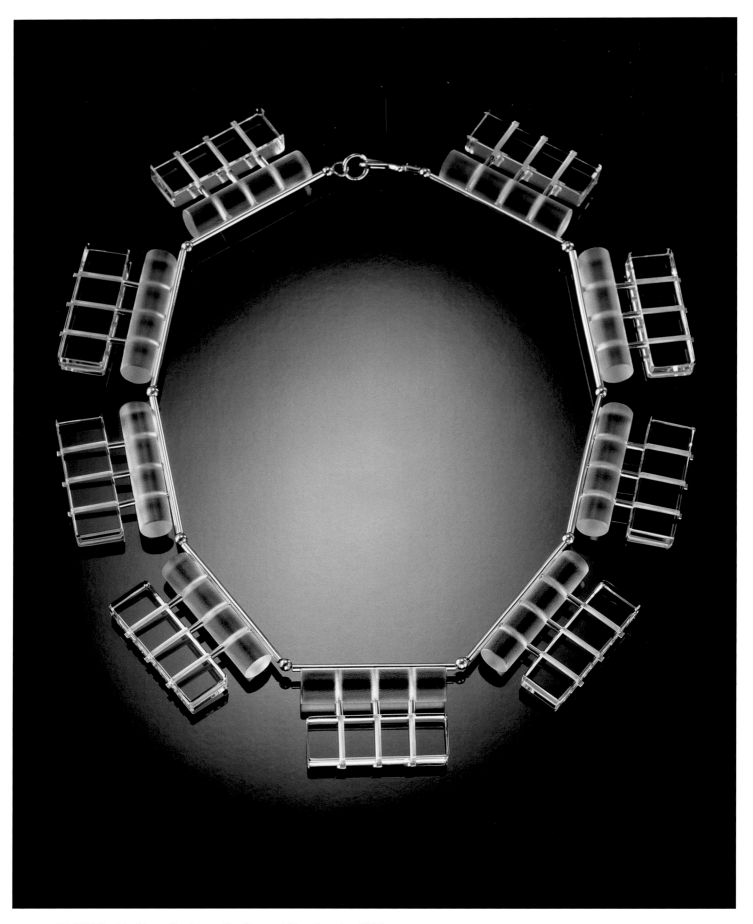

PLATE 8 *Necklace No. 4* from the "Lucent Lines" series, 1984
Plate glass and 14k yellow gold. 20 1/2 x 7/8 x 1/4 inches (52.1 x 2.2 x 0.6 cm) (open)

PLATE 9 *Necklace No. 26* from the "Elements" series, 1984
Cast glass, Vitrolite glass, and 14k yellow gold. 9 3/4 x 7 1/2 x 5/8 inches (24.8 x 19.1 x 1.6 cm) (closed)

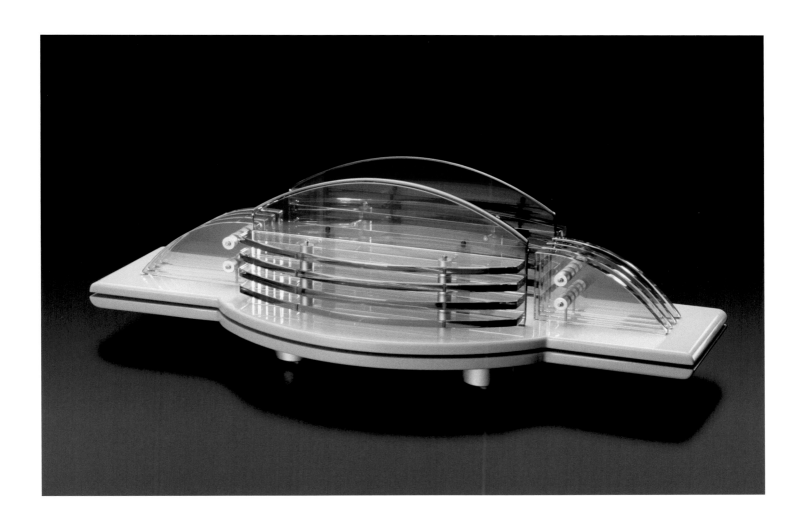

PLATE 10 *Plate Glass Vessel No. 12*, 1984
Vitrolite glass, plate glass, and nickel-plated brass. 5 ³/₄ x 17 ³/₈ x 8 ³/₈ inches (14.6 x 44.1 x 21.3 cm)

PLATE 11 *Neckpiece No. 31* from the "Elements" series, 1985
Vitrolite glass, granite, and 14k yellow gold. 19 x ⅞ x ¾ inches (48.3 x 2.2 x 1.9 cm) (open)

PLATE 12 A–C   *Neck Collar Ensemble No. 1*, ca. 1987
Plate glass, 24k gold–plated brass, and 14k yellow gold

(A) Neck Collar: 6 x 7 x 3/4 inches (15.24 x 17.78 x 1.9 cm)
(B) Bracelet: 4 (dia.) x 1/2 inches (10.2 x 1.3 cm)
(C) Earrings: each 1 x 1/2 x 1/4 inches (2.5 x 1.3 x 0.6 cm)

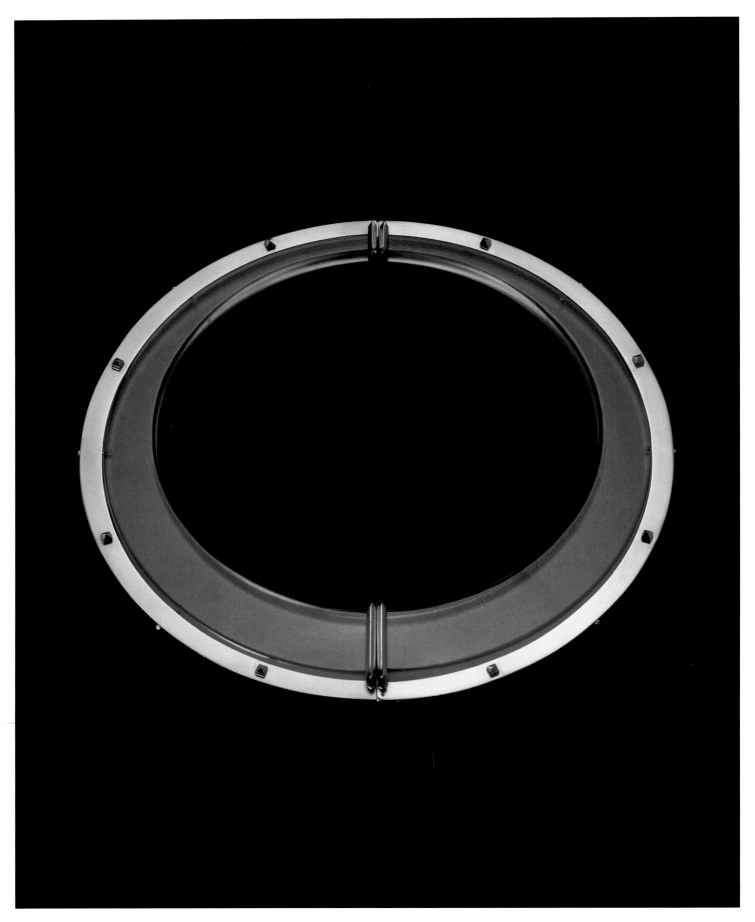

PLATE 13 *Collar No. 3* from the "Neck Collar" series, 1988
Plate glass and 24k gold–plated brass. 8 1/16 x 1 3/8 x 1/2 inches (20.5 x 3.5 x 1.3 cm)

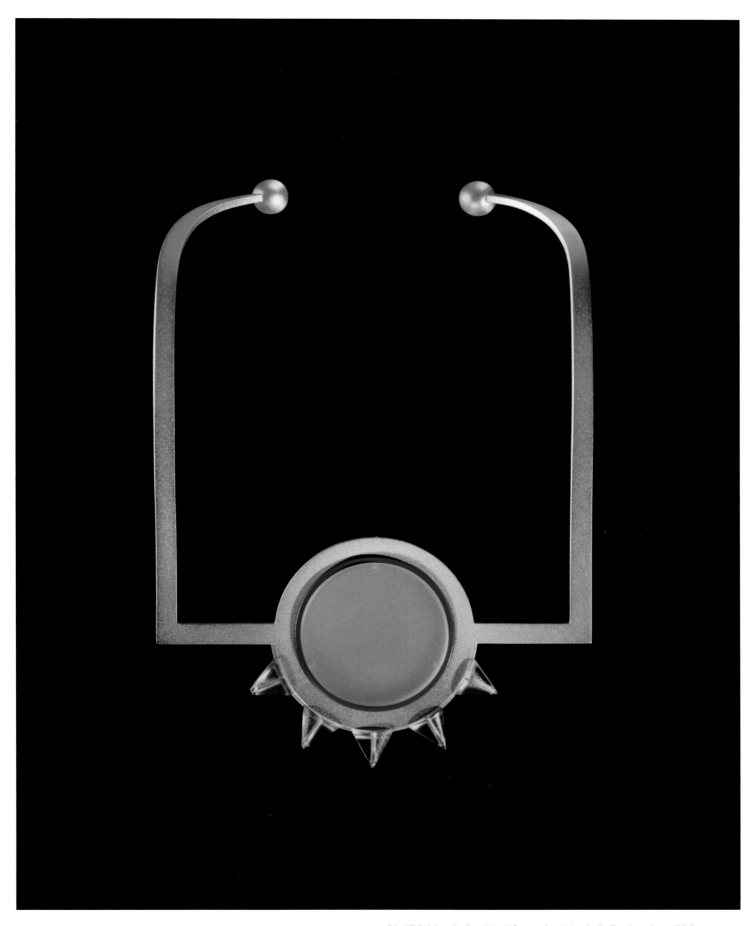

PLATE 14 *Collar No. 7* from the "Neck Collar" series, 1990
Plate glass, enamel paint, and 24k gold-plated brass. 8 x 5 ³/₄ x 2 ¹/₄ inches (20.3 x 14.6 x 5.7 cm)

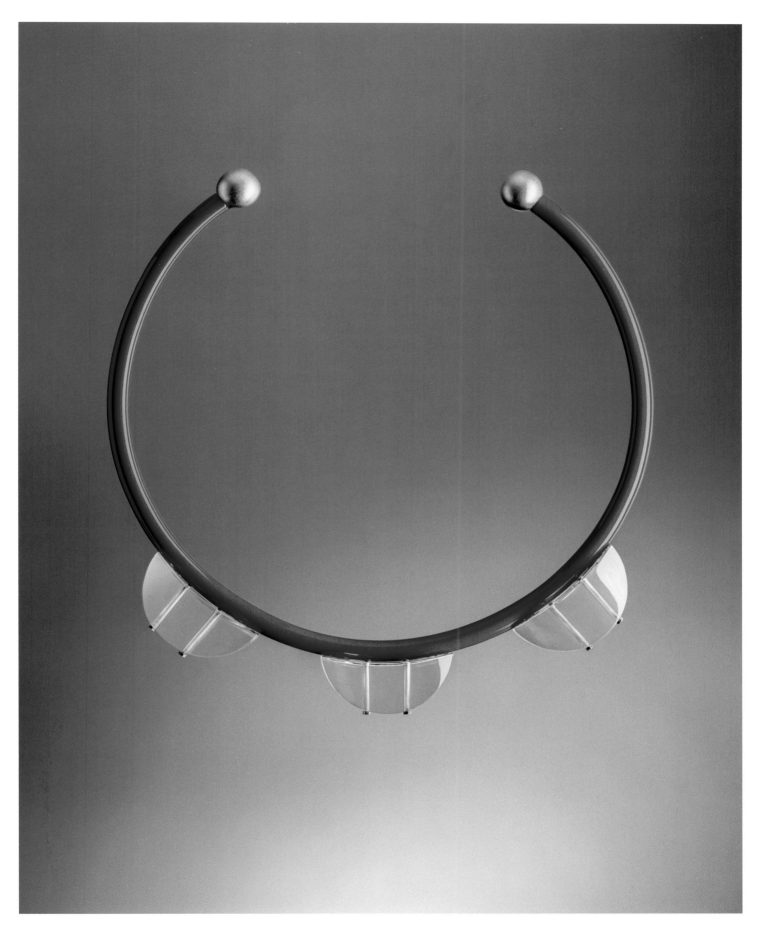

PLATE 15 *Collar No. 9* from the "Neck Collar" series, 1991
Plate glass, enamel paint, aluminum, and 24k gold-plated brass. 6 $\frac{5}{8}$ x 6 $\frac{1}{8}$ x $\frac{3}{8}$ inches (16.8 x 15.6 x 1 cm)

PLATE 16 *Collar No. 10* from the "Neck Collar" series, 1992
Plate glass and 24k gold–plated brass. 5 ³/₄ x 7 ¹/₂ x ³/₄ inches (14.6 x 19.1 x 1.9 cm)

PLATE 17 *Collar No. 12* from the "Neck Collar" series, 1994
Plate glass, mirror, and 24k gold–plated brass. 6 1/2 x 6 1/2 x 1/4 inches (16.5 x 16.5 x 0.6 cm)

PLATE 18 *Necklace No. 1* from the "Mirrored Glass" series, 1994
Plate glass, mirror, and 14k yellow gold. 17 $^3/_4$ x 1 $^1/_{16}$ x $^3/_8$ inches (45.1 x 2.7 x 1 cm) (open)

PLATE 19 *Necklace No. 54* from the "Mesh" series, 1997
Pâte de verre and 24k gold–plated brass. 23 x 3 x ½ inches (58.4 x 7.6 x 1.3 cm) (open)

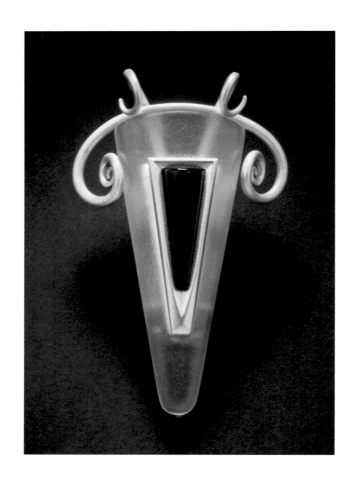

PLATE 20 *Ram's Horn Brooch,* "Brooch" series, no. 1, 1998
Plate glass, Vitrolite glass, and 24k gold–plated brass. 3 $\frac{11}{16}$ x 2 $\frac{5}{16}$ x $\frac{15}{16}$ inches (9.4 x 5.8 x 2.4 cm)

PLATE 21 *Ram's Horn Necklace No. 5*, 1998
Plate glass and 24k gold–plated brass. 6 ⅝ (dia.) x ½ inches (16.8 x 1.3 cm) (closed)

PLATE 22 *Necklace No. 14* from the "Lucent Lines" series, 1999
Plate glass and 14k yellow gold. $20\frac{1}{2}$ x $1\frac{3}{4}$ x $\frac{3}{8}$ inches (52.1 x 4.4 x 1 cm) (open)

PLATE 23 *Lotus Necklace No. 6,* 2000
Lead crystal, plate glass, hot-worked glass, and 14k yellow gold. 16 $\frac{1}{2}$ x 1 $\frac{1}{8}$ x $\frac{3}{8}$ inches (41.9 x 2.9 x 1 cm) (open)

PLATE 24 *Rhombus Fantasy Necklace and Earrings,* "Nexus" series, no. 10, 2000
Plate glass and 24k gold–plated brass
Necklace: 17 1/2 x 4 1/8 x 9/16 inches (44.5 x 10.5 x 1.4 cm) (open)
Earrings: each 1 1/2 x 3/8 x 1/4 inches (3.8 x 1 x 0.6 cm) (not illustrated)

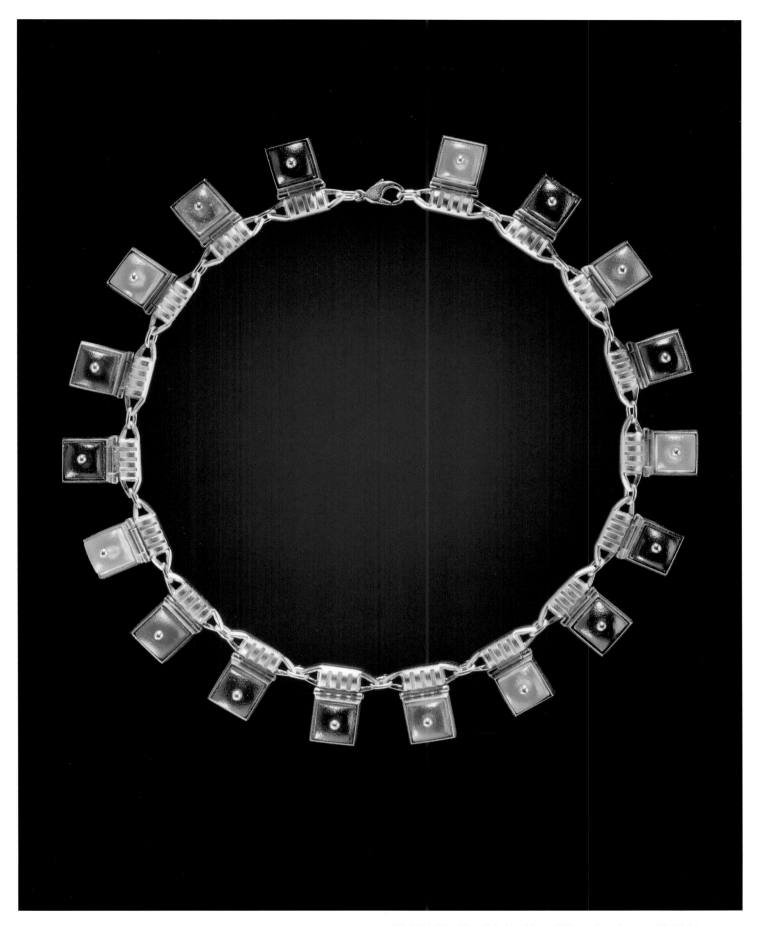

PLATE 25 *Fan Fair Necklace*, "Nexus" series, no. 13, 2001
Plate glass, 24k gold–plated brass, and 14k yellow gold. 16 1/2 x 5/8 x 7/16 inches (41.9 x 1.6 x 1.1 cm) (open)

PLATE 26 *Amber Glow*, "Floral" series, no. 16, 2001–2002
Pâte de verre, plate glass, and 24k gold–plated brass. 23 x 3 x 1¼ inches (58.4 x 7.6 x 3.2 cm) (open)

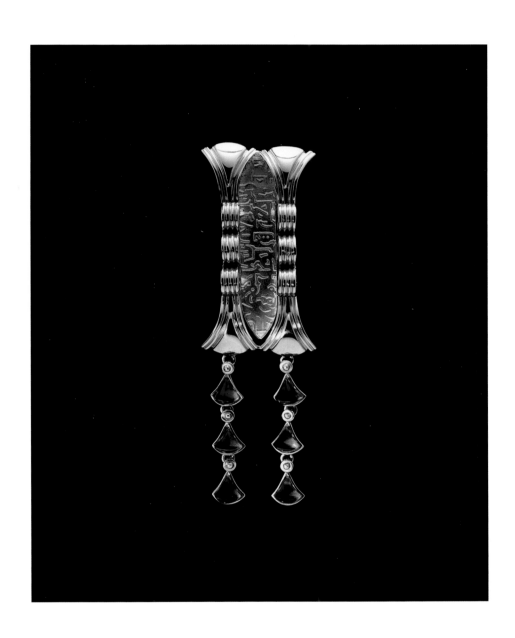

PLATE 27 *According to Legend,* "Brooch" series, no. 17, 2002
Plate glass and 14k yellow gold. 3 ³/₄ x 1 ¹/₄ x ¹/₂ inches (9.5 x 3.2 x 1.3 cm)

PLATE 28 *Egyptian Reed Necklace,* "Floral" series, no. 36, 2003
Pâte de verre, plate glass, mirror, and 24k gold–plated brass. 10 1/2 x 5 13/16 x 3/4 inches (26.7 x 14.8 x 1.9 cm)

PLATE 29 *Sparkling Water Necklace*, "Floral" series, no. 52, 2003–2004
Pâte de verre, plate glass, mirror, diamonds, and platinum. 15 $\frac{1}{2}$ x 2 $\frac{3}{4}$ x $\frac{9}{16}$ inches (39.4 x 7 x 1.4 cm) (open)

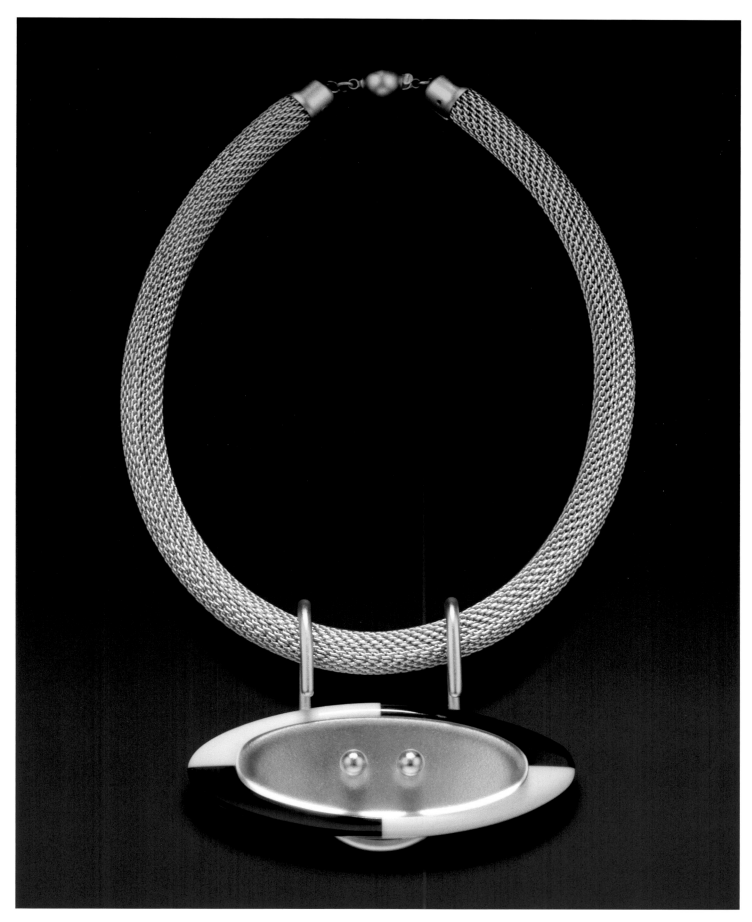

PLATE 30 *Necklace No. 112* from the "Mesh" series, 2004
Plate glass, mirror, Vitrolite glass, and 24k gold-plated brass. 17 5/16 x 2 1/4 x 11/16 inches (44 x 5.7 x 1.7 cm) (open)

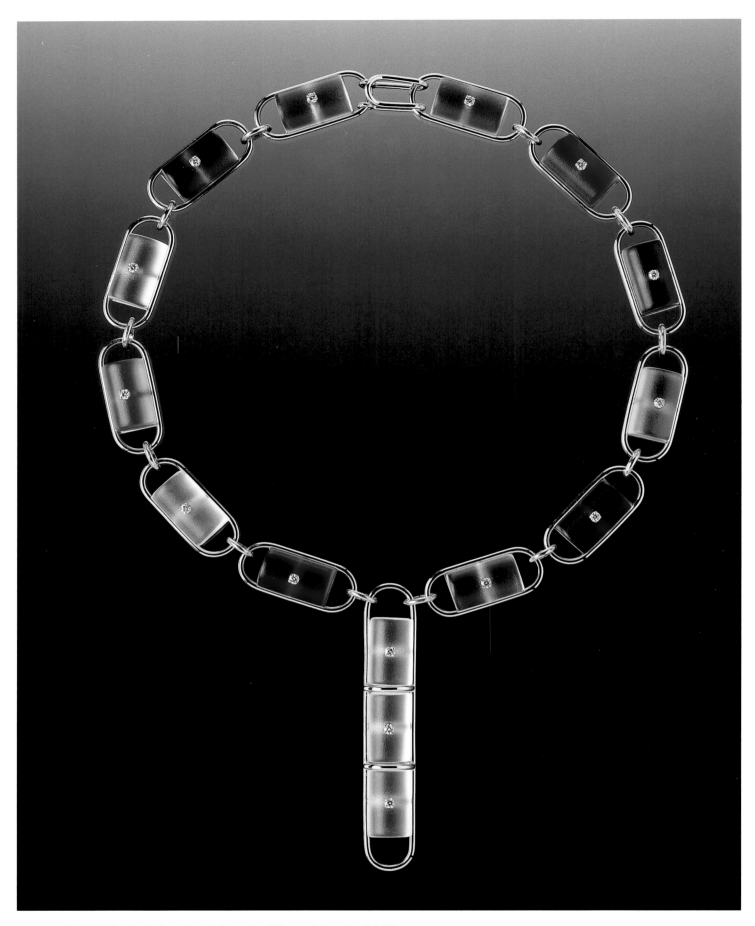

PLATE 31 *Neckpiece No. 40* from the "Elements" series, 2005
Plate glass, mirror, diamonds, and 14k yellow gold. 17 ½ x 3 x ⁷⁄₁₆ inches (44.5 x 7.6 x 1.1 cm) (open)

PLATE 32 *Neckpiece No. 41* from the "Elements" series, 2005
Plate glass, diamonds, and 18k white gold. 6 x 6 x $\frac{7}{16}$ inches (15.2 x 15.2 x 1.1 cm)

PLATE 33 *Ram's Horn*, "Brooch" series, no. 42, 2005
Lead crystal, plate glass, and 18k yellow gold. $1\frac{1}{2} \times 1\frac{1}{4} \times \frac{1}{2}$ inches (3.8 x 3.2 x 1.3 cm)

PLATE 34 *Bouquet Necklace,* "Floral" series, no. 80, 2007
Plate glass, mirror, and 18k yellow gold. 16 $\frac{1}{4}$ x $\frac{7}{8}$ x $\frac{3}{8}$ inches (41.3 x 2.2 x 1 cm) (open)

A   B

LINDA MACNEIL

PLATE 35 *Drawing A/B*, 2006
Pen, ink, and watercolor on paper. 10 $^7/_8$ x 8 $^1/_2$ inches (27.6 x 21.6 cm)

96

PLATE 36 *Luxuriant Blossom Necklace*, "Floral" series, no. 68, 2007
Plate glass, mirror, and 24k gold–plated brass. 19 x 2 ³/₄ x ¹/₂ inches (48.3 x 7 x 1.3 cm) (open)

PLATE 37 *Sublime*, "Brooch" series, no. 80, 2007–13
Plate glass, mirror, and 18k yellow gold. 3 ³/₄ x 2 x ¹/₂ inches (9.5 x 5.1 x 1.3 cm)

DRAWING Ⓑ
VERSION 1

18Y ACTUAL SIZE 3"LONG X 2" WIDTH
GRANULATION

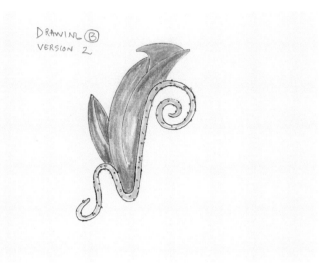

DRAWING Ⓑ
VERSION 2

DRAWING Ⓑ
VERSION 3

DRAWING Ⓑ
VERSION 4

18Y ACTUAL SIZE 3"LONG X 2" WIDTH
GRANULATION

PLATE 38 A–D   *Sublime*, "Brooch" series, no. 80: *Drawing B Versions 1–4*, 2007–13
Photocopy with pencil and colored pencil. Each 4 $\frac{1}{2}$ x 8 $\frac{1}{2}$ inches (11.4 x 21.6 cm)

PLATE 39 *Necklace No. 33* from the "Lucent Lines" series, 2008
Plate glass, mirror, Vitrolite glass, diamonds, and 14k white gold. 17 1/2 x 3 1/8 x 7/16 inches (44.5 x 7.9 x 1.1 cm) (open)

PLATE 40 *Preliminary Drawing: Primavera Necklace,* "Floral" series, no. 98, 2008
Pencil on paper. 14 x 8¼ inches (35.6 x 21 cm)

PLATE 41 *Primavera Necklace*, "Floral" series, no. 98, 2008–16
Plate glass, mirror, diamonds, and 18k yellow gold. 18 x 3 1/4 x 7/16 inches (45.7 x 8.3 x 1.1 cm) (open)

PLATE 42 *Necklace No. 117* from the "Mesh" series, 2008–2009
Plate glass, mirror, diamonds, and 18k white gold. 17 $\frac{1}{2}$ x 2 $\frac{1}{2}$ x $\frac{5}{8}$ inches (44.5 x 6.6 x 1.6 cm) (open)

PLATE 43 *Blue Water Necklace,* "Nexus" series, no. 22, 2010
Plate glass, mirror, 24k gold–plated brass, and 14k yellow gold. 18 x 5 5/16 x 5/16 inches (45.7 x 13.5 x 0.8 cm) (open)

PLATE 44 *Collar No. 17* from the "Neck Collar" series, 2010
Plate glass, mirror, Vitrolite glass, and 24k gold–plated brass. 11 1/4 x 6 1/4 x 3/4 inches (28.6 x 15.9 x 1.9 cm)

PLATE 45 *Collar No. 18* from the "Neck Collar" series, 2010
Plate glass, mirror, Vitrolite glass, and 24k gold–plated brass. 11 $^3/_8$ x 6 $^1/_4$ x $^3/_4$ inches (28.9 x 15.9 x 1.9 cm)

PLATE 46 *Magnificent*, "Brooch" series, no. 78, 2013
Plate glass, mirror, Vitrolite glass, and 18k yellow gold. 4 $\frac{1}{4}$ x 3 $\frac{1}{4}$ x $\frac{3}{8}$ inches (10.8 x 8.3 x 1 cm)

PLATE 47 *Proud,* "Brooch" series, no. 84, 2013
Plate glass, mirror, Vitrolite glass, diamonds, and rhodium-plated 14k white gold. 3 1/4 x 2 3/4 x 5/8 inches (8.3 x 7 x 1.6 cm)

PLATE 48 *Collar No. 23* from the "Neck Collar" series, 2013, modified 2016
Plate glass, mirror, Vitrolite glass, and 24k gold–plated brass. 9 x 5 ³/₄ x ³/₄ inches (22.9 x 14.6 x 1.9 cm)

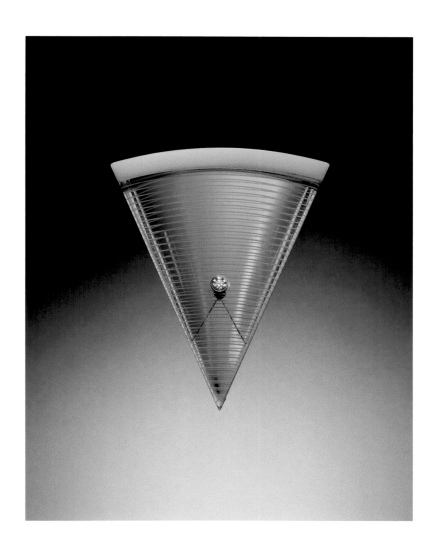

PLATE 49 *Mirrored Brooch*, '"Brooch" series, no. 91, 2015
Cast glass, mirror, Vitrolite glass, diamonds, and 14k white gold. 3 1/16 x 2 1/2 x 1/2 inches (7.8 x 6.4 x 1.3 cm)

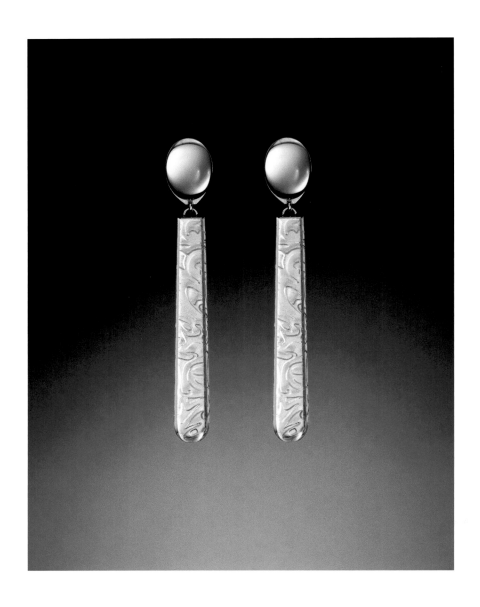

PLATE 50 *Mirrored Earrings No. 15,* 2015
Plate glass, mirror, and rhodium-plated 14k white gold. Each 2 ⁵/₈ x ¹/₄ x ¹/₄ inches (6.7 x 0.6 x 0.6 cm)

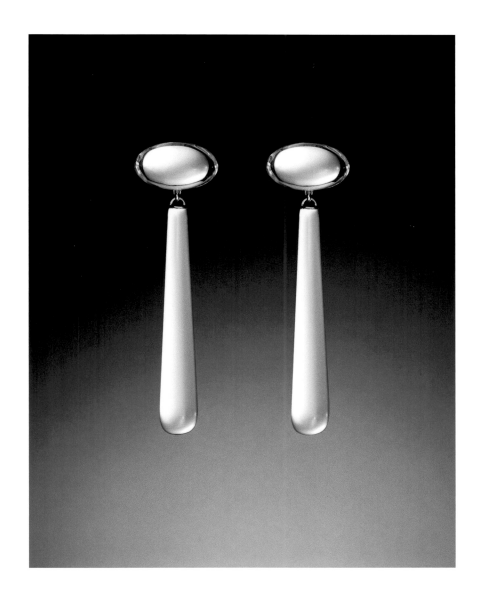

PLATE 51 *Mirrored Earrings No. 16,* 2015
Plate glass, mirror, and rhodium-plated 14k white gold. Each 2 1/2 x 5/8 x 1/4 inches (6.4 x 1.6 x 0.6 cm)

CHRONOLOGY
AND PUBLIC COLLECTIONS

This exhibition history is based upon information provided by the artist and by research gathered from public and private archives. While all efforts have been made to verify the information, in some cases it was not possible to confirm details.

1954
Born Framingham, Massachusetts

EDUCATION

1972–73
Philadelphia College of Art

1973–74
Massachusetts College of Art, Boston

1976
BFA Rhode Island School of Design, Providence

AWARDS/RECOGNITION

1979
Massachusetts Artist Fellowship in Crafts

1984
National Endowment for the Arts Visual Artists' Fellowship, Crafts

2001
The University of the Arts, Philadelphia, Award for Excellence in Jewelry/Metalwork
Coalition of Artists and Collectors Second Annual "Artist as Hero" Award, National Liberty Museum, Philadelphia (with Dan Dailey)

2011
James Renwick Alliance, Master of the Medium, Metal/Jewelry

PROFESSIONAL EXPERIENCE

1976
Studio Assistant, Haystack Mountain School of Crafts, Deer Isle, Maine

1981
Lecture, Boston Glass Works
Lecture, Glass Art Society Conference, Seattle
Visiting Artist, Boston University, School of Artisanry

1982
Visiting Artist, Pilchuck School of Glass, Stanwood, Washington

1985
Lecture, "British Artists in Glass Conference," West Surrey College of Art and Design, Farnham, West Surrey, England (with Dan Dailey)

1986
Lecture, Rhode Island School of Design, Providence (with Dan Dailey)

1989
Lecture, Miasa Bunka Center, Japan (with Dan Dailey)

1999
Participant, Waterford Crystal International Glass Workshop, Kilbarry, Ireland (with Dan Dailey)

2000
Lecture, *The New York Times* InsideCulture Club, "SOFA New York 2000: Sculpture Objects & Functional Art" (with Dan Dailey)
Lecture, Paul Mellon Arts Center Gallery, Choate Rosemary Hall, Wallingford, Connecticut (with Dan Dailey)

2001
Lecture, Beverly Hills Forum Series, Beverly Hills, California (with Dan Dailey)
Lecture, South Shore Art Center, Cohasset, Massachusetts (with Dan Dailey)
Lecture, The University of the Arts, Philadelphia

2002
Artists' panel, Carnegie Museum of Art, Pittsburgh (with Dan Dailey and others)

2003
Lecture, Mint Museum of Craft + Design, Charlotte, North Carolina

2009
Lecture, Memorial Art Gallery—University of Rochester, Rochester, New York

2013
Lecture and Visiting Artist, The University of the Arts, Philadelphia

2011–14
Exhibitions Chair, American Jewelry Design Council, Hermitage, Pennsylvania

2011 ongoing
Member, American Jewelry Design Council, Hermitage, Pennsylvania

SELECTED SOLO EXHIBITIONS

1976
Newton Free Library, Newton Corner, Massachusetts, *Dan Dailey/ Linda MacNeil*

1979
Ten Arrow Gallery, Cambridge, Massachusetts, *Glass Jewelry Combined with Precious Metals*

1980
Julie: Artisans' Gallery, New York, *Glass and Metal Hand Mirrors*

1981
Habatat Galleries, Lathrup Village, Michigan, *Pyramidal Vessels* (parallel solo show for Dan Dailey) (exh. brochure)

1983
David Bernstein Gallery, Boston
Kurland/Summers Gallery, Los Angeles

1984
Habatat Galleries, Bay Harbor Islands, Florida (parallel solo show for Dan Dailey)

1985
Heller Gallery, New York, *Glass Sculpture* (parallel solo show for Dan Dailey)

1986
Anne O'Brien Gallery, Washington, DC, *Constructed Vessels and Jewelry*

1987
Helen Drutt Gallery, Philadelphia, *Contemporary Jewelry*

1988
Helen Drutt Gallery, Philadelphia

1991
Riley Hawk Galleries, Cleveland and Columbus, Ohio (parallel solo show for Dan Dailey)

1993
Riley Hawk Galleries, Cleveland and Columbus, Ohio (parallel solo show for Dan Dailey)

1995
Habatat Galleries, Boca Raton, Florida (parallel solo show for Dan Dailey)
Vespermann Gallery, Atlanta, *Special Collection of Linda MacNeil Glass Necklaces* (parallel solo show for Dan Dailey)

1995–96
Imago Galleries, Palm Desert, California (parallel solo show for Dan Dailey)

1996
Riley Hawk Galleries, Cleveland and Columbus, Ohio, *New Work* (parallel solo show for Dan Dailey)

1997
Habatat Galleries, Boca Raton, Florida, *New Work* (parallel solo show for Dan Dailey)

1998
Riley Hawk Galleries, Cleveland and Columbus, Ohio (parallel solo show for Dan Dailey)

1999
Riley Hawk Galleries, Kirkland, Washington
The Art Center in Hargate, St. Paul's School, Concord, New Hampshire, *Dan Dailey and Linda MacNeil: Art in Glass and Metal* (exh. cat. and video)

2000
Paul Mellon Arts Center Gallery, Choate Rosemary Hall, Wallingford, Connecticut, *Jewelry* (parallel solo show for Dan Dailey)

2001
Habatat Galleries, Boca Raton, Florida (parallel solo show for Dan Dailey)
Riley Hawk Galleries, Cleveland and Columbus, Ohio, and Kirkland, Washington, *Joint Exhibition: Dan Dailey, The Expressive Figure/ Solid Gold & Precious Jewelry of Linda MacNeil*
South Shore Art Center, Cohasset, Massachusetts, *Art in Glass & Metal: Dan Dailey and Linda MacNeil* (exh. brochure)

2003
Mint Museum of Craft + Design, Charlotte, North Carolina, *Sculptural Radiance: The Jewelry & Objects of Linda MacNeil*

2005
Habatat Galleries, Boca Raton, Florida, *Linda MacNeil: Glass & Gold* (parallel solo show for Dan Dailey)

2007
Hawk Galleries, Columbus, Ohio (parallel solo show for Dan Dailey)

2009
Habatat Galleries, Tysons Corner, Virginia (parallel solo show for Dan Dailey)
SOFA West: Santa Fe 2009: Sculpture Objects & Functional Art Fair (with Dan Dailey at Scott Jacobson Gallery) (exh. cat.)

2010
Mobilia Gallery, Cambridge, Massachusetts, *Recent Jewelry* (exh. brochure)
Schantz Galleries Contemporary Glass, Stockbridge, Massachusetts, *Elements of Style: The Sculptural Jewelry of Linda MacNeil* (exh. brochure)

2011
Habatat Galleries, West Palm Beach, Florida, *New Body of Work by Dan Dailey and Linda MacNeil*

2012
Dane Gallery, Nantucket, Massachusetts, *Floral Jewelry: Glass and Precious Metal Jewelry*

2013
Mobilia Gallery, Cambridge, Massachusetts, *Brooches* (exh. brochure)
Sandra Ainsley Gallery, Toronto (parallel solo show for Dan Dailey)

SELECTED GROUP EXHIBITIONS

1975
Colorado State University, Fort Collins, *Contemporary Crafts of the Americas* (exh. cat.)
Cooperstown Art Association, New York, *40th Annual Art Exhibition*

1976
Bruce Gallery, Edinboro State College, Edinboro, Pennsylvania, *Annual National Art Competition 1976 Intent: Jewelry/Metal*
Cooper & French Gallery, Newport, Rhode Island, *Illuminated Glass*
Lever House, New York (organized by Sterling Silversmiths Guild of America), *Statements in Sterling: 1976 Sterling Silver Design Competition*
The Grover M. Hermann Fine Arts Center, Marietta College, Marietta, Ohio, *Marietta College Crafts National '76* (exh. cat.)

1977
Obelisk Gallery, Chestnut Hill, Massachusetts, *Three Jewelers*

1977–79
The Southeastern Center for Contemporary Art, Winston-Salem, North Carolina (with The Museum of Contemporary Crafts of the American Crafts Council, New York), *Young Americans: Fiber, Wood, Plastic, Leather* (exh. cat.; traveled to Contemporary Arts Center, New Orleans; Huntington Galleries, Huntington, West Virginia; Jacksonville Art Museum, Jacksonville, Florida; The Norton Gallery School of Art, West Palm Beach, Florida; The Rochester Institute of Technology, Rochester, New York; The Iowa Art Center, Ames; Hunter Museum of Art, Chattanooga, Tennessee)

1978
Saenger Center, University of Southern Mississippi, Hattiesburg, *The Saenger National Jewelry and Small Sculpture Exhibit* (exh. cat.)
The Creative Arts Workshop, New Haven, Connecticut, *National Metalsmiths Invitational* (exh. cat.)
Theo Portnoy Gallery, New York, *Jewelry by Gallery Artists* (exh. brochure)

1979
Art Gallery, Ball State University, Muncie, Indiana, *Metalworks Invitational 1979* (exh. cat.)
Helen Drutt Gallery, Philadelphia
The Women's Committee of the Philadelphia Museum of Art, *The Philadelphia Craft Show* (exh. brochure)
Rockwell Gallery, Cambridge, Massachusetts, *Clay, Fiber, Metal, Wood, Toys*
The Craftsman's Gallery, Scarsdale, New York, *Art Deco Influence in Contemporary American Crafts*
The Works Gallery, Southampton, New York, *Art Glass '79*
Worcester Craft Center and the Artists Foundation, Worcester, Massachusetts, *Mass. Craft Fellowships*

1980
Huntington Galleries, Huntington, West Virginia, *1980 Glass Art Society Exhibition Catalogue: New American Glass: Focus West Virginia* (exh. cat.)
Gallery of the Center for Music, Drama, and Art, Lake Placid, New York (organized for the XIII Olympic Winter Games by the Museum of Contemporary Crafts, New York, for the National Fine Arts Committee), *Art for Use*
Palo Alto, California (organized for PORTCON '80 conference by *Glass Magazine*, Portland, Oregon), *Fragile Art '80* (exh. brochure)
Shelly Guggenheim, Washington, DC, *Holiday Showing and Sale of Contemporary Museum-Quality Fine Art: Glass/Clay/Fiber/Jewelry*
University of Arizona Museum of Art, Tucson, *Copper 2: The Second Copper, Brass and Bronze Exhibition* (exh. cat.)
University of Delaware, Newark, *Art as Body Adornment* (exh. cat.)

1980–81
Ivor Kurland Gallery, Los Angeles, *Glass: State of the Art*

1981
American Art Gallery, Atlanta, *American Art at Its Best: Glass*
Clark Gallery, Lincoln, Massachusetts, *7 from Glass Routes*
Contemporary Artisans Gallery, San Francisco, *National Glass Invitational*
Contemporary Artisans Gallery, San Francisco, *Viewpoints, Women in Glass*
DeCordova Museum, Lincoln, Massachusetts, *Glass Routes* (exh. cat.)

1981–82
Leigh Yawkey Woodson Art Museum, Wausau, Wisconsin, *Americans in Glass* (exh. cat.; traveled to The Cooper-Hewitt Museum, The Smithsonian Institution's National Museum of Design, New York; Krannert Art Museum, University of Illinois at Urbana-Champaign; Bergstrom Art Center and Mahler Glass Museum, Neenah, Wisconsin)

1981–84
Bass Museum of Art, Miami Beach, Florida (organized by the Smithsonian Institution Traveling Exhibition Service), *Good as Gold: Alternative Materials in American Jewelry* (exh. cat.; traveled to Renwick Gallery, National Museum of American Art, Smithsonian Institution, Washington, DC; Dallas Historical Society; Oglebay Institute, Wheeling, West Virginia; State University of New York [SUNY], New Paltz; San Jose Museum of Art, San Jose, California; Tacoma Art Museum, Tacoma, Washington; Daytona Beach Community College, Daytona Beach, Florida; Muskegon Museum of Art, Muskegon, Michigan; Ontario Crafts Council, Toronto; McAllen International Museum, McAllen, Texas; Leigh Yawkey Woodson Museum, Wausau, Wisconsin; University of Delaware, Newark; Museums at Sunrise, Charleston, West Virginia; Museo La Tertulia, Cali, Columbia; Binational Center, La Paz; Binational Center, Asuncíon, Paraguay; Museo Nacional de Bellas Artes, Santiago; Binational Center, Lima)

1982
Contemporary Artisans Gallery, San Francisco, *National Glass IV*
Hatabat Galleries, Lathrup Village, Michigan, *10th Annual National Exhibition*
HumanArts, Dallas, *Masters in Glass*
Traver Sutton Gallery, Seattle, *Pilchuck Glass*
Young Gallery, San Jose, California, *Contemporary American Glass*

1982–83
The Art Gallery of Western Australia, Perth, *Glass: International Directions in Glass Art* (exh. cat.; traveled to state art museums in Victoria, Queensland, New South Wales, and Tasmania)

1983
Contemporary Artisans Gallery, San Francisco, *National Glass V*
Habatat Galleries, Lathrup Village, Michigan, *The 11th Annual National Invitational of Contemporary American Glass* (exh. cat.; traveled to Columbus College of Art and Design, Columbus, Ohio; work not included in tour)

Tucson Museum of Art, Tucson, Arizona, *Sculptural Glass* (exh. cat.; traveled to Owens-Illinois World Headquarters Building, Toledo, Ohio)
American Embassy Residence, Prague (organized by The Corning Museum of Glass, Corning, New York), *Contemporary American Glass Sculpture* (exh. cat.)

1984
Habatat Galleries, Lathrup Village, Michigan, *Contemporary Glass: National—International* (exh. cat., traveled to Owens-Illinois Arts Center, Toledo, Ohio)

1984–86
American Craft Museum II, New York (organized by the American Craft Museum), *Jewelry USA* (exh. cat.; traveled to Virginia Museum of Fine Arts, Richmond; Craft & Folk Art Museum, Los Angeles; The Chicago Public Library Cultural Center; The Oakland Museum, Oakland, California; Hunter Museum of Art, Chattanooga, Tennessee; Bass Museum of Art, Miami Beach, Florida; National Ornamental Metal Museum, Memphis; Newport Art Museum, Newport, Rhode Island)

1985
David Bernstein Gallery, Boston, *Carrie Harper, Linda MacNeil, Marsha & Kurt Runstadler*
Elaine Potter Gallery, San Francisco, *Glass '85*
Habatat Galleries, Lathrup Village, Michigan, *The Thirteenth Annual National Glass Invitational* (exh. brochure)
Le Musée des Beaux-Arts de Rouen, France (co-organized with L'Association Renouveau du Verre en Haute-Normandie, *Art du Verre: Actualité internationale* (exh. cat.)
Quadrum Gallery, Chestnut Hill, Massachusetts, *Worked with Gold II*

1985–86
Habatat Galleries, Bay Harbor, Florida, *Glass: The New Aesthetic*

1985–87
American Craft Museum, New York, *American Jewelry Now* (exh. cat.; traveled to Thomas Jefferson Cultural Center, Makati, Philippines; Joong-Aug Gallery, Seoul; National Museum of History, Taipei; National Museum, Jakarta; National Museum, Singapore; National Museum, Kuala Lumpur; Auckland City Art Gallery; Robert McDougall Art Gallery, Christchurch, New Zealand)

1986
Bevier Gallery of Art, Rochester Institute of Technology, Rochester, New York, *Architecture of the Vessel* (exh. cat.)
Contemporary Crafts Gallery, Portland, Oregon, *Invitational Glass Exhibition* (juried by LaMar Harrington)
Cross Creek Gallery, Malibu, California, *American Glass Sampler*
Habatat Galleries, Lathrup Village, Michigan, *The 14th Annual National Glass Invitational* (exh. cat.)
Huntington Galleries, Huntington, West Virginia, *New American Glass: Focus 2 West Virginia* (exh. cat.)
Nina Owen, Ltd., Chicago, *Sculptors from the New York Experimental Glass Workshop*

1986–87
The Society for Art in Crafts, Pittsburgh, *Contemporary Crafts: A Concept in Flux* (exh. cat.)

1986–88
American Craft Museum, New York, *Craft Today: Poetry of the Physical* (exh. cat.; traveled to The Denver Art Museum; Laguna Art Museum, Laguna Beach, California; Milwaukee Art Museum;

J. B. Speed Art Museum, Louisville, Kentucky; Virginia Museum of Fine Arts, Richmond)

1987
Chicago International New Art Forms Exposition 1987 (with Helen Drutt Gallery) (exh. cat.)
Habatat Galleries, Lathrup Village, Michigan, *Glass Gems III*

1987–88
Habatat Galleries, Bay Harbor Islands, Florida, *The New Aesthetic: A Worldwide Survey of Contemporary Glass Sculpture*

1988
Chicago International New Art Forms Exposition 1988 (with Helen Drutt Gallery) (exh. cat.)
Florida State University Fine Arts Gallery & Museum, Tallahassee, and Habatat Galleries, Inc., Bay Harbor Islands, Florida, *A Generation in Glass Sculpture* (exh. cat.)
Habatat Galleries, Lathrup Village, Michigan, *The 16th Annual International Glass Invitational* (exh. cat.)
Helen Drutt Gallery, New York, *Work in Progress: A Preview June 9–July 31, 1988*
The Hand and the Spirit, Scottsdale, Arizona, *Women in Glass: The New Spirit*

1989
Habatat Galleries, Boca Raton, Florida, *The Eighth Annual International Glass Invitational* (exh. brochure)

1989–93
American Craft Museum, New York, *Craft Today USA* (exh. cat.; traveled to Musée des Arts Décoratifs, Paris; Taidetollisuusmuseoi, Helsinki; Museum für Kunsthandwerk, Frankfurt; Zachęta State Gallery of Art, Warsaw; Musée des Arts Décoratifs, Lausanne; All-Russia Museum of Decorative, Applied and Folk Art, Moscow; State Painting and Sculpture Museum, Ankara; Kunstindustrimuseet, Oslo; St. Peter's Abbey, Ghent; America Haus, Berlin; Zappeion, Athens; Slovak National Gallery, Bratislava; Grassi Museum, Leipzig; Sala Sant Jaume de la Fundacio "La Caixa," Barcelona; Museu Calouste Gulbenkian, Lisbon)

1990
Facèré Jewelry Salon, Seattle, *glass wear*
Vespermann Gallery, Atlanta, *Holiday Glass Show*

1990–91
American Craft Museum, New York, *Selections from the Permanent Collection*

1991
Wheeler/Seidel Gallery, New York, *Contemporary Jewelry*

1992–93
Habatat Shaw Gallery, Farmington Hills, Michigan, *Precious Art to Wear: An Exquisite Collection of Contemporary Jewelry*

1993
Chicago International New Art Forms Exposition 1993 (with The Jewelry Project) (exh. cat.)
Wheaton Village, Millville, New Jersey, *GlassWeekend '93: A Symposium & Exhibition of Contemporary Glass* (organized by the Art Alliance for Contemporary Glass, The Corning Museum of Glass, and The Creative Glass Center of America (with The Jewelry Project, *The Glass Jewel*) (exh. cat.)
Helander Gallery, Palm Beach, Florida, *Sculptural/Functional Show*

1993–95
Toledo Museum of Art, Toledo, Ohio, *Contemporary Crafts and the Saxe Collection* (exh. cat.; traveled to The St. Louis Art Museum; Newport Harbor Art Museum, Newport Beach, California; Renwick Gallery of the National Museum of American Art, Smithsonian Institution, Washington, DC)

1994
Miller Gallery, New York, *To Wear and To View: Sculpture and Jewelry in Glass and Mixed Media*
Miller Gallery, New York, *First Annual International Invitational Jewelry Exhibition*
Mobilia Gallery, Cambridge, Massachusetts, *Invitational Jewelry Exhibition*
SOFA 1994 Exposition: Sculpture Objects & Functional Art, Chicago (with Miller Gallery and Leo Kaplan Modern) (exh. cat.)

1995
SOFA Chicago Exposition 1995: Sculpture Objects Functional Art (with Leo Kaplan Modern) (exh. cat.)
SOFA Miami Exposition 1995: Sculpture Objects Functional Art (with Miller Gallery) (exh. cat.)

1995–96
Mobilia Gallery, Cambridge, Massachusetts, *Art Jewelry: An Historical View*

1996
Charles A. Wustum Museum of Fine Arts, Racine, Wisconsin, *The Brillson Foundation: American Glass of the 1980s* (exh. brochure)
Clark Gallery, Lincoln, Massachusetts, *Glass: The Cutting Edge*
SOFA Chicago Exposition 1996: Sculpture Objects Functional Art (with Leo Kaplan Modern) (exh. cat.)
SOFA Miami Exposition 1996: Sculpture Objects Functional Art (with Leo Kaplan Modern) (exh. cat.)

1997
Wheaton Village, Millville, New Jersey, *GlassWeekend '97* (with Leo Kaplan Modern) (exh. cat.)
Det Danske Kunstindustrimuseum, Copenhagen (co-organized with the American Craft Museum), *Celebrating American Craft 1975–1995* (exh. cat.)
SOFA Exposition Chicago 1997: Sculpture Objects Functional Art (with Leo Kaplan Modern) (exh. cat.)
SOFA Miami Exposition 1997: Sculpture Objects Functional Art (with Leo Kaplan Modern) (exh. cat.)

1997–98
Habatat Galleries, Boca Raton, Florida, *15th International Glass Invitational* (exh. cat.)

1998
SOFA Chicago 1998: Sculpture Objects Functional Art (with Leo Kaplan Modern) (exh. cat.)
SOFA New York 1998: Sculpture Objects Functional Art (with Leo Kaplan Modern) (exh. cat.)

1998–99
Habatat Galleries, Boca Raton, Florida, *16th Annual International Glass Invitational* (exh. cat.)

1998–2001
American Craft Museum, New York, *Craft Is a Verb: Selections from the Collection of the American Craft Museum* (traveled to Mississippi Museum of Art, Jackson; Sarah Moody Gallery, University of Alabama, Tuscaloosa; Sunrise Museum, Charleston,

West Virginia; Miami University Gallery, Oxford, Ohio; Tampa Museum of Art, Tampa, Florida)

1999
Wheaton Village, Millville, New Jersey, *GlassWeekend '99* (with Leo Kaplan Modern) (exh. cat.)
Grand Central Gallery, Tampa, Florida, *New Perspectives/Ancient Medium: A Survey of Sculptural Glass from the Traditional to the Experimental*
SOFA Chicago 1999: Sculpture Objects Functional Art (with Leo Kaplan Modern) (exh. cat.)
SOFA 1999 NYC: Sculpture Objects Functional Art (with Leo Kaplan Modern) (exh. cat.)

1999–2000
Mobilia Gallery, Cambridge, Massachusetts, *50 Years of Studio Jewelry: A Survey of Contemporary Work from the 1950s to the Present*
Renwick Gallery of the Smithsonian's American Art Museum, Washington, DC, *Glass! Glorious Glass!* (exh. brochure)

2000
American Craft Museum, New York, *Defining Craft I: Collecting for the New Millennium*
Mobilia Gallery, Cambridge, Massachusetts, *Structure, Symbol & Substance: The Power of Jewelry*
SOFA Chicago 2000: The Seventh Annual International Exposition of Sculpture Objects & Functional Art (with Leo Kaplan Modern) (exh. cat)
SOFA New York 2000: Sculpture Objects & Functional Art (with Leo Kaplan Modern) (exh. cat.)

2000–2001
Habatat Galleries, Boca Raton, Florida, *Contemporary Glass 2001: Eighteenth Annual International Glass Invitational* (exh. cat.)
Kentucky Art and Craft Foundation, Louisville, *Millennium Glass: An International Survey of Studio Glass* (exh. cat.; traveled to Montgomery Museum of Fine Arts, Montgomery, Alabama; Hunter Museum of American Art, Chattanooga, Tennessee)

2001
Habatat Galleries, Boca Raton, Florida, *The Nineteenth Annual International Glass Invitational* (exh. cat.)
Mobilia Gallery, Cambridge, Massachusetts, *Hot Glass*
SOFA Chicago 2001: Sculpture Objects & Functional Art (with Leo Kaplan Modern) (exh. cat.)

2002
SOFA Chicago 2002: The International Exposition of Sculpture Objects & Functional Art (with Leo Kaplan Modern) (exh. cat.)
SOFA New York 2002: The Fifth Annual International Exposition of Sculpture Objects & Functional Art (with Leo Kaplan Modern) (exh. cat.)

2002–2003
Habatat Galleries, Boca Raton, Florida, *Contemporary Glass 2003: Twentieth Annual International Glass Invitational* (exh. cat.)

2002–2004
Carnegie Museum of Art, Pittsburgh, and Toledo Museum of Art, Toledo, Ohio, *Contemporary Directions: Glass from the Maxine and William Block Collection* (exh. cat.)

2003
Mobilia Gallery, Cambridge, Massachusetts, *Botanical Jewelry*
SOFA Chicago 2003: The Tenth Annual Exposition of Sculpture

Objects & Functional Art (with Leo Kaplan Modern) (exh. cat.)
SOFA New York 2003: The Sixth Annual Exposition of Sculpture Objects & Functional Art (with Leo Kaplan Modern) (exh. cat.)

2003–2004
Habatat Galleries, Boca Raton, Florida, *Contemporary Glass 2004: Twenty-First Annual International Glass Invitational* (exh. cat.)
Smithsonian American Art Museum, Renwick Gallery, Washington, DC, *Jewels & Gems* (exh. brochure)

2003–2005
Society of North American Goldsmiths, Lisle, Illinois, *The Art of Gold* (exh. cat.; traveled by ExhibitsUSA to Crocker Art Museum, Sacramento, California; University of Richmond Museums, Richmond, Virginia; Arkansas Arts Center, Little Rock; The Mint Museum of Craft + Design, Charlotte, North Carolina; Anchorage Museum, Alaska)

2004
Fuller Craft Museum, Brockton, Massachusetts, *The Perfect Collection: A Shared Vision for Contemporary Craft* (exh. cat.)
Mobilia Gallery, Cambridge, Massachusetts, *Historical Connections: A Group Exhibition*
SOFA Chicago 2004: The Eleventh Annual International Exposition of Sculpture Objects & Functional Art (with Leo Kaplan Modern) (exh. cat.)
SOFA New York 2004: The Seventh Annual International Exposition of Sculpture Objects & Functional Art (with Leo Kaplan Modern) (exh. cat.)

2004–2005
American Craft Museum, New York, *Treasures from the Vault: Jewelry from the Permanent Collection*
Habatat Galleries, Boca Raton, Florida, *Contemporary Glass 2005: Twenty-Second Annual International Glass Invitational* (exh. cat.)

2005
Charles A. Wustum Museum of Fine Arts, Racine, Wisconsin (organized by Racine Art Museum), *Magnificent Extravagance: Artists and Opulence* (exh. brochure)
Museum of American Glass at Wheaton Village, Millville, New Jersey, *Particle Theories: International Pâte de Verre and Other Cast Glass Granulations* (exh. cat.)
SOFA Chicago 2005: The Twelfth Annual Exposition of Sculpture Objects & Functional Art (with Leo Kaplan Modern) (exh. cat.)
SOFA New York 2005: The Eighth Annual International Exposition of Sculpture Objects & Functional Art (with Leo Kaplan Modern) (exh. cat.)

2005–2006
Habatat Galleries, Boca Raton, Florida, *Contemporary Glass 2006: 23rd Annual International Glass Invitational* (exh. cat.)

2006
Alfred Berkowitz Gallery, University of Michigan-Dearborn, *Women's Glass from Michigan Artists and Collections*
ArtPalmBeach 2006, West Palm Beach, Florida (with Leo Kaplan Modern) (exh. cat.)
Habatat Galleries, Boca Raton, Florida, *Contemporary Glass 2007: The 24th Annual International Glass Invitational* (exh. cat)
SOFA Chicago 2006: The Thirteenth Annual International Exposition of Sculpture Objects & Functional Art (with Leo Kaplan Modern) (exh. cat.)
SOFA New York 2006: The Ninth International Exposition of Sculpture Objects & Functional Art (with Leo Kaplan Modern) (exh. cat.)

Worcester Center for Crafts, Worcester, Massachusetts, *New England Glass: The Quiet Force* (exh. cat.)

2006–2009
Helen Drutt: Philadelphia, and Designmuseo, Helsinki, *Challenging the Châtelaine!* (exh. cat.; traveled to Tarbekunstimuuseum, Tallinn, Estonia; Lalaounis Jewelry Museum, Athens; Design Museum, Ghent, Belgium; Stedelijk Museum 's-Hertogenbosch, 's-Hertogenbosch, the Netherlands; Philadelphia Art Alliance)

2007
Mobilia Gallery, Cambridge, Massachusetts, *Celebrating the Art of Adornment: Studio Jewelry from Mid-Century to Present*
SOFA Chicago 2007: The Fourteenth Annual International Exposition of Sculpture Objects & Functional Art (with Leo Kaplan Modern) (exh. cat.)
SOFA New York 2007: The Tenth International Exposition of Sculpture Objects & Functional Art (with Leo Kaplan Modern) (exh. cat.)
Wheaton Arts and Cultural Center, Millville, New Jersey, *GlassWeekend '07* (with Leo Kaplan Modern) (exh. cat.)

2007–10
Glass Pavilion, Toledo Museum of Art, Toledo, Ohio (organized by Museum of Arts & Design, New York, and Schmuckmuseum Pforzheim, Pforzheim, Germany), *GlassWear: Glass in Contemporary Jewelry* (exh. cat.; traveled to Glazen Huis Vlaams Centrum voor Hedendaagse Glaskunst, Lommel, Belgium; Art Museum of South Texas, Corpus Christi; Memorial Art Gallery—University of Rochester, Rochester, New York; Mobile Museum of Art, Mobile, Alabama; Southeastern Center for Contemporary Art, Winston-Salem, North Carolina)

2008
Mobilia Gallery, Cambridge, Massachusetts, *Glass Quake 2008*
Mobilia Gallery, Cambridge, Massachusetts, *Ahead of Its Time: Jewelry in the Milieu of 1900*
SOFA Chicago 2008: The Fifteenth Anniversary Sculpture Objects & Functional Art Fair (with Leo Kaplan Modern) (exh. cat)
SOFA New York 2008: The 11th Annual Sculpture Objects & Functional Art Fair (with Leo Kaplan Modern) (exh. cat.)
Victoria and Albert Museum, London, *William and Judith Bollinger Jewellery Gallery*

2008–2009
Museum of Arts and Design, New York, *Elegant Armor: The Art of Jewelry* (exh. cat.)

2009
Wheaton Arts and Cultural Center, Millville, New Jersey (with Scott Jacobson Gallery), *GlassWeekend '09: An International Symposium and Exhibition of Contemporary Glass* (organized by Creative Glass Center of America and the Art Alliance for Contemporary Glass) (exh. cat.)
SOFA Chicago 2009: The Sixteenth Annual Sculpture Objects & Functional Art Fair (with Scott Jacobson Gallery) (exh. cat)
SOFA New York 2009: The 12th Annual Sculpture Objects & Functional Art Fair (with Leo Kaplan Modern) (exh. cat.)

2009–10
Habatat Galleries, West Palm Beach, Florida, *Contemporary Glass 2010: 27th Annual International Glass Invitational* (exh. cat.)
Mobilia Gallery, Cambridge, Massachusetts, *Heirlooms of the Future, Jewelry, Holloware & Sculpture*

2010
Fine Arts Gallery, Lake Placid Center for the Arts, Lake Placid, New York, *Precious Metals, Jewelry & Functional Art*
Racine Art Museum, Racine, Wisconsin, *A Glass Act: First Rate Glass from RAM's Collection*
SOFA Chicago 2010: Sculpture Objects & Functional Art Fair (with Scott Jacobson Gallery) (exh. cat.)
SOFA New York 2010: The 13th Annual Sculpture Objects & Functional Art Fair (with Scott Jacobson Gallery) (exh. cat.)
SOFA West: Santa Fe 2010: Sculpture Objects & Functional Art Fair (with Scott Jacobson Gallery) (exh. cat.)
Kentucky Museum of Art and Craft, Louisville, *Glass Jewelry: An International Passion*

2010–11
Habatat Galleries, West Palm Beach, Florida, *2011 Palm Beach Contemporary Glass: 28th Annual Glass Invitational* (exh. cat.)
The Montreal Museum of Fine Arts, *Studio Glass: Anna and Joe Mendel Collection* (exh. cat.)

2011
Mobilia Gallery, Cambridge, Massachusetts, *Glass Quake 2011* (exh. brochure)
Mobilia Gallery, Cambridge, Massachusetts, *Objects of Status, Power and Adornment: The Studio Jewelry Movement 1950–2011*
SOFA Chicago 2011: Sculpture Objects & Functional Art Fair (with Wexler Gallery) (exh. cat.)

2012
Mobilia Gallery, Cambridge, Massachusetts, *Contemporary Visions of the Necklace, Part I*
SOFA Art & Design New York 2012 (with Wexler Gallery) (exh. cat.)

2012–13
Mobilia Gallery, Cambridge, Massachusetts, *Art for the Ear/The Art of the Ring*
Museum of Arts and Design, New York, *Playing with Fire: 50 Years of Contemporary Glass*
Racine Art Museum, Racine, Wisconsin, *The Cutting Edge: RAM Honors 50 Years of Studio Art Glass Jewelry* (exh. brochure)

2013
Pôle Bijou Galerie, Baccarat, France, *Rêves de verre* (exh. brochure)_
SOFA Art and Design Chicago 2013: The 20th Annual Sculpture Objects Functional Art + Design Fair (with Hawk Galleries) (exh. cat.; traveled to Hawk Galleries, Columbus, Ohio)

2013–16
The Forbes Gallery, New York (organized by the American Jewelry Design Council), *Variations on a Theme: 25 Years of Designs from the AJDC* (exh. cat.; traveled to Alumni Gallery, Kent State University Museum, Kent, Ohio; JCK Las Vegas, Las Vegas, Nevada; Gemological Institute of America, Carlsbad, California)

2014
Mint Museum Uptown, Charlotte, North Carolina, *Allure of Flowers: Botanical Motifs in Craft, Design, and Fashion* (organized by The Mint Museum)
New Britain Museum of American Art, New Britain, Connecticut, *Glass Today: 21st-Century Innovations* (exh. cat.)

2015
Asheville Art Museum, Asheville, North Carolina, *Flourish: Selected Jewelry from the Daphne Farago Collection*

Mobilia Gallery, Cambridge, Massachusetts, *A Journey Through Time: Explorations of Artful Adornment & Sculptural Vessels Through the Ages*
Museum of Arts and Design, New York, *Jewelry* curated by Isabel and Ruben Toledo in *Ralph Pucci: The Art of the Mannequin* (exh. cat.; not in catalogue)

2015–16
Racine Art Museum, Racine, Wisconsin, *Standing on Ceremony: Functional Ware from RAM's Collection* (exh. brochure)

2016
Glass Pavilion, Toledo Museum of Art, Toledo, Ohio, *Hot Spot: Contemporary Glass from Private Collections*

PUBLIC COLLECTIONS

American Jewelry Design Council, Hermitage, Pennsylvania
Les Archives de la Cristallerie Daum, Nancy and Paris
The Cleveland Museum of Art
Corning Museum of Glass, Corning, New York
Currier Museum of Art, Manchester, New Hampshire
Detroit Institute of Arts
Gemological Institute of America, Carlsbad, California
Los Angeles County Museum of Art
The Metropolitan Museum of Art, New York
The Mint Museum, Charlotte, North Carolina
The Montreal Museum of Fine Arts
Museum of Art, Rhode Island School of Design, Providence
Museum of Arts and Design (formerly American Craft Museum), New York
Museum of Fine Arts, Boston
The Museum of Fine Arts, Houston
Philadelphia Museum of Art
Racine Art Museum, Racine, Wisconsin
Smithsonian American Art Museum, Washington, DC
Speed Museum, Louisville, Kentucky
Toledo Museum of Art, Toledo, Ohio
Victoria and Albert Museum, London

SELECTED BIBLIOGRAPHY

Ariail, Kate Dobbs. "Reviews: Sculptural Radiance: The Jewelry and Objects of Linda MacNeil, Mint Museum of Craft + Design, Charlotte, North Carolina, August 9–November 23, 2003." *Metalsmith* 24, 3 (Summer 2004), p. 48.

Becker, Vivienne. *Art Nouveau Jewelry*. New York: Thames & Hudson, 1985.

Bernstein, Rosita. "Glas Schmuck—Glass Jewelry—Bijoux de Verre." *Neues Glas* 1 (January–March 1986), pp. 36–44.

Bernstein, Ruby. "Sculptural Glass: The Tucson Museum of Art 1983 Glass Art Exhibition." *American Art Glass Quarterly*, Fall 1983, pp. 68–79.

Besten, Liesbeth den. *On Jewellery: A Compendium of International Contemporary Art Jewellery*. Stuttgart: Arnoldsche Art Publishers, 2011.

Bizot, Chantal. "Bijoux de verre, un tour d'horizon." *La Revue de la céramique et du verre* 28 (May–June 1986), cover, pp. 16–22.

Byrd, Joan Falconer. "Review: Linda MacNeil/Mint Museum of Craft + Design, Charlotte, NC, August 9–November 23, 2003." *American Craft* 64, 1 (February–March 2004), pp. 78–79.

Chambers, Karen S. "Linda MacNeil: A Detailed Look." *Metalsmith* 16, 3 (Summer 1996), pp. 24–33.

Cocordas, Eleni. "Linda MacNeil: Helen Drutt Gallery, Philadelphia, Pa." *Metalsmith* 9, 1 (Winter 1989), p. 48.

Cooper, Michele. "Illuminated Glass, Cooper & French, Newport, Rhode Island, August 28–September 15." *Craft Horizons* 36, 6 (December 1976), p. 59.

Cummings, Keith. *Contemporary Kiln-formed Glass*. London and Philadelphia: A&C Black Publishers and University of Pennsylvania Press, 2009, pp. 71, 85, 88, 89, 128–29.

Cummins, Susan. "Linda MacNeil: Brooches," interview with the artist by Susan Cummins, Art Jewelry Forum, http://www.artjewelryforum.org/ajf-blog/linda-macneil-brooches, July 27, 2013.

English, Helen W. Drutt, and Peter Dormer. *Jewelry of Our Time: Art, Ornament and Obsession*. New York: Rizzoli International Publications, Inc., 1995, pp. 337–38.

Falino, Jeannine, ed. *Crafting Modernism: Midcentury American Art and Design*. New York: Harry N. Abrams, 2012.

Frantz, Susanne K. *Contemporary Glass: A World Survey from The Corning Museum of Glass*. New York: Harry N. Abrams, Inc. Publishers, 1989, p. 94.

Friedman, Jane. "Kindred Spirits." *AmericanStyle*, Summer 2002, pp. 68–77.

Gregorietti, Guido. *Jewelry through the Ages*. New York: Crescent Books, 1969.

Hampson, Ferdinand, ed. *Glass: State of the Art 1984*. Huntington Woods, Michigan: Elliott Johnston Publishers, 1984, pp. 62–63.

Hampson, Ferdinand. *Insight: A Collector's Guide to Contemporary American Glass*. Huntington Woods, Michigan: Elliott Johnston Publishers, 1985, unpaginated, chapter 3.

Hemachandra, Ray. *Showcase 500 Art Necklaces* (juried by Chunghi Choo). New York: Lark Crafts, 2013, p. 271.

Ilse-Neuman, Ursula. "The Glamour of Glass Jewelry." *Glass* 109 (Winter 2007–2008), pp. 42–49. Adapted from Ilse-Neuman, Ursula, Cornelie Holzach, and Jutta-Annette Page. *GlassWear: Glass in Contemporary Jewelry*. Stuttgart: Arnoldsche Art Publishers in collaboration with the Museum of Arts & Design, New York, and the Schmuckmuseum Pforzheim, Pforzheim, Germany, 2007.

———. *Inspired Jewelry from the Museum of Arts and Design*. New York and Woodbridge, England: Museum of Arts and Design in association with ACC Editions, 2009, pp. 17, 180, 210.

Khani, Layla. "Linda MacNeil Jewellery." *Visual Masters*, Winter 2011, pp. 42–55, www.vmmag.co.uk.

Klein, Dan. *Glass: A Contemporary Art*. New York: Rizzoli, 1989, p. 71.

———. "Linda MacNeil." Unpublished manuscript, 1987. Linda MacNeil Archives, New Hampshire, 1987.

Klotz, Uta M. "Linda MacNeil: Wearable Art." *Neues Glas* 4 (Winter 2003), pp. 10–17.

Kohler, Lucartha. *Women Working in Glass*. Atglen, Pennsylvania: Schiffer Publishing Ltd., 2003, pp. 115–20, 153–54.

Kuroki, Rika. "Interview: Linda MacNeil." *Glasswork* 3 (October 1989), pp. 16–21.

Le Van, Marthe. *21st Century Jewelry: The Best of the 500 Series*. New York: Lark Crafts, 2011, pp. 229, 410.

———, ed. *500 Brooches: Inspiring Adornments for the Body* (juried by Marjorie Simon). New York: Lark Books, 2005, p. 67.

———, ed. *500 Necklaces: Contemporary Interpretations of a Timeless Form* (juried by Marjorie K. Schick). New York: Lark Books, 2006, p. 415.

Lewin, Susan Grant, et al. *One of a Kind: American Art Jewelry Today*. New York: Harry N. Abrams, 1994.

Lieberman, Elizabeth Broadrup. "Commissions." *Metalsmith* 23, 2 (Spring 2003), p. 42.

Liu, Robert K. "Publication Reviews: Mostly Glass." *Ornament* 28, 2 (2004), pp. 70–71.

Liu, Robert K., and James Minson. "Contemporary Glass Jewelry: A Continuing Tradition." *Ornament* 24, 3 (Spring 2001), pp. 40–45.

Lonier, Terri. "Jewelry as Wearable Art." *The Robb Report* 8, 8 (August 1984), pp. 50–57.

———. "Linda MacNeil: Artistic Innovation in Glass." *Neues Glas* 2 (1985), cover, pp. 60–66.

MacNeil, Linda. "Artists' Statements: Linda MacNeil." *Glass Art Society Journal*, 1981, pp. 54–55.

Magon, Birgit. "Die US-Schmuckgestalterin Linda MacNeil: One + One = One." *Kunst + Handwerk* 10 (October 1981), pp. 425–26.

Markowitz, Yvonne J. *Artful Adornments: Jewelry from the Museum of Fine Arts, Boston*. Boston: Museum of Fine Arts, 2011, pp. 180–81.

Meilach, Dona Z. *Art Jewelry Today*. Atglen, Pennsylvania: Schiffer Publishing Ltd., 2003, pp. 178–79.

Michelson, Maureen, ed. "Introducing Fragile Art '80." *Glass Magazine* 9, 1 (January 1982), pp. 17–66.

Miller, Bonnie. "A Matter of Scale: Innovations in American Glass Jewelry." *Glasswork* 15 (July 1993), pp. 18–25.

Mills, Rosie Chambers, and Bobbye Tigerman, eds. *Beyond Bling: Contemporary Jewelry from the Lois Boardman Collection* (Los Angeles and New York: Los Angeles County Museum of Art and DelMonico Books/Prestel, 2016).

Minson, James. "Fragile Enhancements." *Glass* 52 (Summer 1993), pp. 38–43.

Mouillefarine, Laurence, and Evelyne Possémé. *Art Deco Jewelry: Modernist Masterworks and their Makers*. New York: Thames & Hudson, 2009.

New Glass Review 1. Corning, New York: The Corning Museum of Glass, 1980, p. 9.

New Glass Review 2. Corning, New York: The Corning Museum of Glass, 1981, p. 7.

New Glass Review 3. Corning, New York: The Corning Museum of Glass, 1982, pp. 2, 11.

New Glass Review 17. Corning, New York: The Corning Museum of Glass, 1996, pp. 75, 89. Included in *Neues Glas* 2 (1996).

New Glass Review 20. Corning, New York: The Corning Museum of Glass, 1999, p. 92. Included in *Neues Glas* 2 (1999).

New Glass Review 25. Corning, New York: The Corning Museum of Glass, 2004, pp. 30, 51.

New Glass Review 32. Corning, New York: The Corning Museum of Glass, 2011, p. 114.

Newman, Harold. *An Illustrated Dictionary of Jewelry: 2530 Terms Relating to Gemstones, Jewels, Materials, Processes, Styles, Designers, and Makers from Antiquity to the Present Day*. London: Thames and Hudson, 1999.

Norton, Deborah. "A History of the School for American Craftsmen." *Metalsmith* 5, 1 (Winter 1985), pp. 14–21.

Oldknow, Tina, with foreword by Thomas S. Buechner. *25 Years of New Glass Review*. Corning, New York: The Corning Museum of Glass, 2005, pp. 209–10, 223, 244.

———, with artist's biography by Margery Aronson. *Linda MacNeil: Original and Unique Works in Waterford Crystal*. Kilbarry, Waterford, Ireland: Waterford Wedgewood, PLC, n.d.

Perry, Pamela. "Exhibitions: Boston: David Bernstein Gallery." *Craft International*, July/August/September 1985, pp. 40–41.

"Portfolio: Linda MacNeil." *American Craft* 40, 1 (February–March 1980), p. 45.

Ramljak, Suzanne, and Helen W. Drutt English. *United in Beauty: The Jewelry and Collectors of Linda MacNeil*. Atglen, Pennsylvania: Schiffer Publishing Ltd., 2002.

Skinner, Damian, ed. *Contemporary Jewelry in Perspective*. New York: Sterling Publishing, 2013.

Stern, Robert A. M., ed. *The International Design Yearbook 1985/86*. New York: Abbeville Press, Publishers, 1985, pp. 130–31, 224.

Strauss, Cindi, with Helen Williams Drutt English, Keelin M. Burrows, and Kristen Wetzel. *Ornament as Art: Avant-Garde Jewelry from the Helen Williams Drutt Collection, The Museum of Fine Arts, Houston*. Stuttgart and Houston: Arnoldsche Art Publishers in association with The Museum of Fine Arts, Houston, 2007, pp. 394, 486.

Wheaton, Hazel L. "A Conversation with Linda MacNeil." *Art Jewelry* 8, 2 (January 2012), pp. 40–42.

Woell, J. Fred. "Linda MacNeil: New Work, David Bernstein Gallery, Boston, MA." *Metalsmith* 3, 4 (Fall 1983), p. 47.

CATALOGUE
OF THE EXHIBITION

All works of art in this exhibition were carefully researched by the guest curator in conjunction with the artist; the captions reflect their findings. The chronological presentation has been tweaked to position drawings adjacent to finished works.

PLATE 1 A–B
Necklace and Bracelet from the "Elements" series, ca. 1979
Plate glass, sterling silver, and 14k yellow gold
(A) Necklace: 18 x $^7/_8$ x 1 inches (45.7 x 2.2 x 2.5 cm) (open)
(B) Bracelet: 8 $^{15}/_{16}$ x $^3/_4$ x $^7/_8$ inches (22.7 x 1.9 x 2.2 cm) (open)
Collection of Joan and Jay Ochroch
Photo by John Carlano Photography

PLATE 2
Neckpiece No. 2 from the "Elements" series, 1979
Vitrolite glass and 14k yellow gold
19 $^1/_2$ x 2 $^1/_4$ x $^3/_8$ inches (49.53 x 5.7 x 1 cm) (open)
Collection of the Philadelphia Museum of Art, purchased with funds contributed by The Women's Committee and the Craft Show Committee of the Philadelphia Museum of Art, 2008
Photo by Susie Cushner

PLATE 3
Hand Mirror No. 15, 1979–81
Vitrolite glass, mirror, plate glass, found glass tubing, and 24k gold-plated brass
8 x 12 x 4 inches (20.3 x 30.5 x 10.2 cm)
Courtesy of the artist
Photo by Michael Tropea, Chicago

PLATE 4
Hand Mirror No. 11, 1980
Hot-worked glass, Vitrolite glass, and 24k gold-plated brass
12 x 6 x 4 inches (30.5 x 15.2 x 10.2 cm)
Lent by the Corning Museum of Glass, Corning, New York
Photo by Susie Cushner

PLATE 5
Neckpiece No. 20 from the "Elements" series, 1982
Vitrolite glass, plate glass, and 14k yellow gold
16 x 1 x $^3/_8$ inches (40.6 x 2.5 x 1 cm) (open)
Courtesy of the artist
Photo © Bill Truslow Photography

PLATE 6
Neckpiece No. 22 from the "Elements" series, 1983
Hot-worked glass, plate glass, and 14k yellow gold
15 $^1/_4$ x 1 $^1/_4$ x $^7/_{16}$ inches (38.7 x 3.2 x 1.1 cm) (open)
Collection of Anne and Ronald Abramson
Photo by Michael Tropea, Chicago

PLATE 7
Necklace No. 3 from the "Lucent Lines" series, 1983
Plate glass and 14k yellow gold
23 $^1/_2$ x 1 x $^1/_4$ inches (59.7 x 2.5 x 0.6 cm) (open)
Collection of Joan and Jay Ochroch
Photo by John Carlano Photography

PLATE 8
Necklace No. 4 from the "Lucent Lines" series, 1984
Plate glass and 14k yellow gold
20 $^1/_2$ x $^7/_8$ x $^1/_4$ inches (52.1 x 2.2 x 0.6 cm) (open)
Collection of Joan and Jay Ochroch
Photo by Susie Cushner

PLATE 9
Necklace No. 26 from the "Elements" series, 1984
Cast glass, Vitrolite glass, and 14k yellow gold
9 $^3/_4$ x 7 $^1/_2$ x 5/8 inches (24.8 x 19.1 x 1.6 cm) (closed)
Collection of the Los Angeles County Museum of Art, gift of Lois and Bob Boardman
Photo © Museum Associates/ LACMA

PLATE 10
Plate Glass Vessel No. 12, 1984
Vitrolite glass, plate glass, and nickel-plated brass
5 $^3/_4$ x 17 $^3/_8$ x 8 $^3/_8$ inches (14.6 x 44.1 x 21.3 cm)
Collection of Anne and Ronald Abramson
Photo by Susie Cushner

PLATE 11
Neckpiece No. 31 from the "Elements" series, 1985
Vitrolite glass, granite, and 14k yellow gold
19 x 7/8 x $^3/_4$ inches (48.3 x 2.2 x 1.9 cm) (open)
Courtesy of the artist
Photo by Michael Tropea, Chicago

PLATE 12 A–C
Neck Collar Ensemble No. 1, ca. 1987
Plate glass, 24k gold-plated brass, and 14k yellow gold
(A) Neck Collar: 6 x 7 x $^3/_4$ inches (15.24 x 17.78 x 1.9 cm)
(B) Bracelet: 4 (dia.) x $^1/_2$ inches (10.2 x 1.3 cm)
(C) Earrings: each 1 x $^1/_2$ x $^1/_4$ inches (2.5 x 1.3 x 0.6 cm)
Lent by the Corning Museum of Glass, Corning, New York
Photo courtesy of the Corning Museum of Glass

PLATE 13
Collar No. 3 from the "Neck Collar" series, 1988
Plate glass and 24k gold-plated brass
8 $^1/_{16}$ x 1 $^3/_8$ x $^1/_2$ inches (20.5 x 3.5 x 1.3 cm)
Collection of the Philadelphia Museum of Art, purchased with funds contributed by The Women's Committee and the Craft Show Committee of the Philadelphia Museum of Art, 2008
Photo © Charles Mayer Photography

PLATE 14
Collar No. 7 from the "Neck Collar" series, 1990
Plate glass, enamel paint, and 24k gold-plated brass
8 x 5 $^3/_4$ x 2 $^1/_4$ inches (20.3 x 14.6 x 5.7 cm)
Collection of the Museum of Arts and Design, New York, museum purchase with funds provided by Chris Rifkin and the Collections Committee, 2000
Photo © Charles Mayer Photography

PLATE 15
Collar No. 9 from the "Neck Collar" series, 1991
Plate glass, enamel paint, aluminum, and 24k gold-plated brass
6 $^5/_8$ x 6 $^1/_8$ x $^3/_8$ inches (16.8 x 15.6 x 1 cm)
Courtesy of the artist
Photo © Bill Truslow Photography

PLATE 16
Collar No. 10 from the "Neck Collar" series, 1992
Plate glass and 24k gold-plated brass
5 3/4 x 7 1/2 x 3/4 inches
(14.6 x 19.1 x 1.9 cm)
Courtesy of the artist
Photo by Michael Tropea, Chicago

PLATE 17
Collar No. 12 from the "Neck Collar" series, 1994
Plate glass, mirror, and 24k gold-plated brass
6 1/2 x 6 1/2 x 1/4 inches
(16.5 x 16.5 x 0.6 cm)
Courtesy of the artist
Photo by Michael Tropea, Chicago

PLATE 18
Necklace No. 1 from the "Mirrored Glass" series, 1994
Plate glass, mirror, and 14k yellow gold
17 3/4 x 1 1/16 x 3/8 inches
(45.1 x 2.7 x 1 cm) (open)
Collection of Anna and Joe Mendel
Photo by Denis Farley, courtesy of The Montreal Museum of Fine Arts

PLATE 19
Necklace No. 54 from the "Mesh" series, 1997
Pâte de verre and 24k gold-plated brass
23 x 3 x 1/2 inches
(58.4 x 7.6 x 1.3 cm) (open)
Courtesy of the artist
Photo © Bill Truslow Photography

PLATE 20
Ram's Horn Brooch, "Brooch" series, No. 1, 1998
Plate glass, Vitrolite glass, and 24k gold-plated brass
3 11/16 x 2 5/16 x 15/16 inches
(9.4 x 5.8 x 2.4 cm)
Collection of The Montreal Museum of Fine Arts, gift of Anna and Joe Mendel
Photo by Christine Guest, courtesy of The Montreal Museum of Fine Arts

PLATE 21
Ram's Horn Necklace No. 5, 1998
Plate glass and 24k gold-plated brass
6 5/8 (dia.) x 1/2 inches

(16.8 x 1.3 cm) (closed)
Courtesy of the artist
Photo © Bill Truslow Photography

PLATE 22
Necklace No. 14 from the "Lucent Lines" series, 1999
Plate glass and 14k yellow gold
20 1/2 x 1 3/4 x 3/8 inches
(52.1 x 4.4 x 1 cm) (open)
Collection of Joan and Jay Ochroch
Photo by John Carlano Photography

PLATE 23
Lotus Necklace No. 6, 2000
Lead crystal, plate glass, hot-worked glass, and 14k yellow gold
16 1/2 x 1 1/8 x 3/8 inches
(41.9 x 2.9 x 1 cm) (open)
Courtesy of the artist
Photo © Bill Truslow Photography

PLATE 24
Rhombus Fantasy Necklace and Earrings, "Nexus" series, No. 10, 2000
Plate glass and 24k gold-plated brass
Necklace: 17 1/2 x 4 1/8 x 9/16 inches
(44.5 x 10.5 x 1.4 cm) (open)
Earrings: each 1 1/2 x 3/8 x 1/4 inches (3.8 x 1 x 0.6 cm) (not illustrated)
Courtesy of the artist
Photo by Michael Tropea, Chicago

PLATE 25
Fan Fair Necklace, "Nexus" series, No. 13, 2001
Plate glass, 24k gold-plated brass, and 14k yellow gold
16 1/2 x 5/8 x 7/16 inches
(41.9 x 1.6 x 1.1 cm) (open)
Collection of Chris Rifkin
Photo © Bill Truslow Photography

PLATE 26
Amber Glow, "Floral" series, No. 16, 2001–2002
Pâte de verre, plate glass, and 24k gold-plated brass
23 x 3 x 1 1/4 inches
(58.4 x 7.6 x 3.2 cm) (open)
Collection of Colleen and John Kotelly
Photo by Michael Tropea, Chicago

PLATE 27
According to Legend, "Brooch" series, No. 17, 2002
Plate glass and 14k yellow gold
3 3/4 x 1 1/4 x 1/2 inches
(9.5 x 3.2 x 1.3 cm)
Courtesy of the artist
Photo © Bill Truslow Photography

PLATE 28
Egyptian Reed Necklace, "Floral" series, No. 36, 2003
Pâte de verre, plate glass, mirror, and 24k gold-plated brass
10 1/2 x 5 13/16 x 3/4 inches
(26.7 x 14.8 x 1.9 cm)
Collection of Giselle and Benjamin Huberman
Photo by Lunardi Photography

PLATE 29
Sparkling Water Necklace, "Floral" series, No. 52, 2003–2004
Pâte de verre, plate glass, mirror, diamonds, and platinum
15 1/2 x 2 3/4 x 9/16 inches
(39.4 x 7 x 1.4 cm) (open)
Collection of Klara Silverstein
Photo by Michael Tropea, Chicago

PLATE 30
Necklace No. 112 from the "Mesh" series, 2004
Plate glass, mirror, Vitrolite glass, and 24k gold-plated brass
17 5/16 x 2 1/4 x 11/16 inches
(44 x 5.7 x 1.7 cm) (open)
Collection of The Montreal Museum of Fine Arts, gift of the artist
Photo by Christine Guest, courtesy of The Montreal Museum of Fine Arts

PLATE 31
Neckpiece No. 40 from the "Elements" series, 2005
Plate glass, mirror, diamonds, and 14k yellow gold
17 1/2 x 3 x 7/16 inches
(44.5 x 7.6 x 1.1 cm) (open)
Courtesy of the artist
Photo © Bill Truslow Photography

PLATE 32
Neckpiece No. 41 from the "Elements" series, 2005
Plate glass, diamonds, and 18k white gold
6 x 6 x 7/16 inches

(15.2 x 15.2 x 1.1 cm)
Collection of the Museum of Arts and Design, New York, gift of Mrs. Nanette L. Laitman, 2016
Photo © Bill Truslow Photography

PLATE 33
Ram's Horn, "Brooch" series, No. 42, 2005
Lead crystal, plate glass, and 18k yellow gold
1 1/2 x 1 1/4 x 1/2 inches
(3.8 x 3.2 x 1.3 cm)
Collection of Diane and Marc Grainer
Photo © Bill Truslow Photography

PLATE 34
Bouquet Necklace, "Floral" series, No. 80, 2007
Plate glass, mirror, and 18k yellow gold
16 1/4 x 7/8 x 3/8 inches
(41.3 x 2.2 x 1 cm) (open)
Collection of Joan and Alvin Einbender
Photo © Bill Truslow Photography

PLATE 35
Drawing A/B, 2006
Pen, ink, and watercolor on paper
10 7/8 x 8 1/2 inches
(27.6 x 21.6 cm)
Collection of the Linda MacNeil Archives, New Hampshire
Photo © Bill Truslow Photography

PLATE 36
Luxuriant Blossom Necklace, "Floral" series, No. 68, 2007
Plate glass, mirror, and 24k gold-plated brass
19 x 2 3/4 x 1/2 inches
(48.3 x 7 x 1.3 cm) (open)
Collection of Ellie and Mark Lainer
Photo © Bill Truslow Photography

PLATE 37
Sublime, "Brooch" series, No. 80, 2007–13
Plate glass, mirror, and 18k yellow gold
3 3/4 x 2 x 1/2 inches
(9.5 x 5.1 x 1.3 cm)
Courtesy of the artist
Photo © Bill Truslow Photography

PLATE 38 A-D
Sublime, "Brooch" series,
No. 80: *Drawing B Versions 1–4*,
2007–13
Photocopy with pencil and
colored pencil
Each 4 1/2 x 8 1/2 inches
(11.4 x 21.6 cm)
Collection of the Linda MacNeil
Archives, New Hampshire
Photo courtesy of the artist

PLATE 39
Necklace No. 33 from the
"Lucent Lines" series, 2008
Plate glass, mirror, Vitrolite
glass, diamonds, and 14k white
gold
17 1/2 x 3 1/8 x 7/16 inches
(44.5 x 7.9 x 1.1 cm) (open)
Collection of Diane and Jerome
Phillips
Photo by Michael Tropea,
Chicago

PLATE 40
*Preliminary Drawing: Primavera
Necklace*, "Floral" series,
No. 98, 2008
Pencil on paper
14 x 8 1/4 inches (35.6 x 21 cm)
Collection of the Linda MacNeil
Archives, New Hampshire
Photo © Bill Truslow
Photography

PLATE 41
Primavera Necklace, "Floral"
series, No. 98, 2008–16
Plate glass, mirror, diamonds,
and 18k yellow gold
18 x 3 1/4 x 7/16 inches
(45.7 x 8.3 x 1.1 cm) (open)
Courtesy of the artist
Photo by Michael Tropea,
Chicago

PLATE 42
Necklace No. 117 from the
"Mesh" series, 2008–2009
Plate glass, mirror, diamonds,
and 18k white gold
17 1/2 x 2 1/2 x 5/8 inches
(44.5 x 6.6 x 1.6 cm) (open)
Collection of Marian and
Russell Burke
Photo by Michael Tropea,
Chicago

PLATE 43
Blue Water Necklace, "Nexus"
series, No. 22, 2010
Plate glass, mirror, 24k gold–
plated brass, and 14k yellow
gold
18 x 5 5/16 x 5/16 inches

(45.7 x 13.5 x 0.8 cm) (open)
Courtesy of the artist
Photo by Michael Tropea,
Chicago

PLATE 44
Collar No. 17 from the "Neck
Collar" series, 2010
Plate glass, mirror, Vitrolite
glass, and 24k gold-plated
brass
11 1/4 x 6 1/4 x 3/4 inches
(28.6 x 15.9 x 1.9 cm)
Courtesy of the artist
Photo by Michael Tropea,
Chicago

PLATE 45
Collar No. 18 from the "Neck
Collar" series, 2010
Plate glass, mirror, Vitrolite
glass, and 24k gold-plated
brass
11 3/8 x 6 1/4 x 3/4 inches
(28.9 x 15.9 x 1.9 cm)
Collection of Colleen and John
Kotelly
Photo by Michael Tropea,
Chicago

PLATE 46
Magnificent, "Brooch" series,
No. 78, 2013
Plate glass, mirror, Vitrolite
glass, and 18k yellow gold
4 1/4 x 3 1/4 x 3/8 inches
(10.8 x 8.3 x 1 cm)
Courtesy of the artist
Photo © Bill Truslow
Photography

PLATE 47
Proud, "Brooch" series, No. 84,
2013
Plate glass, mirror, Vitrolite
glass, diamonds, and rhodium-
plated 14k white gold
3 1/4 x 2 3/4 x 5/8 inches
(8.3 x 7 x 1.6 cm)
Courtesy of the artist
Photo © Bill Truslow
Photography

PLATE 48
Collar No. 23 from the "Neck
Collar" series, 2013, modified
2016
Plate glass, mirror, Vitrolite
glass, and 24k gold-plated
brass
9 x 5 3/4 x 3/4 inches
(22.9 x 14.6 x 1.9 cm)
Collection of Diane and Jerome
Phillips
Photo by Michael Tropea,
Chicago

PLATE 49
Mirrored Brooch, "Brooch"
series, No. 91, 2015
Cast glass, mirror, Vitrolite
glass, diamonds, and 14k white
gold
3 1/16 x 2 1/2 x 1/2 inches
(7.8 x 6.4 x 1.3 cm)
Courtesy of the artist
Photo © Bill Truslow
Photography

PLATE 50
Mirrored Earrings No. 15, 2015
Plate glass, mirror, and
rhodium-plated 14k white gold
Each 2 5/8 x 1/4 x 1/4 inches
(6.7 x 0.6 x 0.6 cm)
Courtesy of the artist
Photo © Bill Truslow
Photography

PLATE 51
Mirrored Earrings No. 16, 2015
Plate glass, mirror, and
rhodium-plated 14k white gold
Each 2 1/2 x 5/8 x 1/4 inches
(6.4 x 1.6 x 0.6 cm)
Courtesy of the artist
Photo © Bill Truslow
Photography